Outgrowing
Self-Deception

OUTGROWING
SELF-DECEPTION

GARDNER MURPHY

WITH MORTON LEEDS

BASIC BOOKS, INC., Publishers

NEW YORK

Library of Congress Cataloging in Publication Data

Murphy, Gardner, 1895–
  Outgrowing self-deception.

  Bibliography: p.
  Includes index.
    1. Self-deception. 2. Self-perception. I. Leeds,
  Morton, joint author. II. Title.
  BF697.M85   155.2   74–79277
  ISBN 0–465–05390–4

To Charles M. Solley

CONTENTS

———

[vii]

Contents

PREFACE

PERCEIVING IS A SKILL. We think of fencing and embroidery as crafts, but perceiving is a craft, too—indeed, a craft upon which the wielding of the foil or the needle depends. The tea taster and the wine sampler detect the nuances of aroma and bouquet that others miss; they cut through the perceptual "haze." The musician's "ear" is not anatomical but refers to his skill in apprehending.

Though personally without musical gift, I learned to "hear" music in an adolescent experience. For four years in college, I dutifully attended symphony concerts but did not "hear" them. Then, one evening I sat at the very tip of the tilted horseshoe in the balcony of Carnegie Hall, and was able to look straight down at the cellist and watch the fingering of the woodwinds. Identifying the instruments as I picked them out against the background of full orchestration, I found that I could perceive music. Ever afterward, having gone through this phase of perceptual learning, I could "hear."

It is different with each of us, but whatever our cultural and family background of hearing or unhearing, seeing or unseeing, we have had a lot of perceptual learning to do be-

[xi]

fore the world of "chance," "love," and "logic" could be sorted out and we learned to see it, hear it, as it is.

Or do we see the world as we like to believe it is? Did we learn, as a junior member of a clan, to perceive in a clan-determined way, as rock musicians have learned to hear differently from the baroque masters, the great romanticists, and the atonal experimentalists? Or was it at times a matter of climbing through a long tunnel all alone, confident that there was something to be seen that we had not yet seen, perhaps that had never been seen?

Or are there different *ways* of seeing? Did a moment of surprise, a "peak in Darien" experience, provide a new way of seeing that had been possible but never realized? Or in discovering a new way, have doubts developed about it, producing oscillation between two ways? Have any of us reached a point where we threw up our hands in despair, doubting whether ultimate truth was attainable; or have we, sweeping aside all timid and escapist theories, declared like Dr. Johnson, banging the table, that there is a solid reality after all?

In our quest for truth, we may have discovered a world of mounting uncertainties, which, bedeviling us and magnifying our wishes and fears, made us feel ensnared. Perhaps we gradually discovered that habits, desires, fears, and cultural standards do not control our perceptions completely, but that we adjust everything to our own picture of reality. Perhaps, like the British zoologist teaching her medical students how to read X rays, we decided that we must investigate the "anatomy of judgment" if we are to reach a high level of faith in our capacity to understand. Or perhaps, if we are as modern as we think we are, we have reached the point at which James Gibson has arrived—believing that the senses are really concerned with the processing of information and that it is the biophysical effectiveness or ineffectiveness of this processing that must replace the ancient problem of "truth" versus "error."

Even if we reach such a point, we know that self-deception

is still there, involving wishful thinking and a dependence upon our own needs and fears, keeping us from reality day and night. We may begin to wonder if there is any way of clearing out the junk of self-deception or of achieving a slightly higher level of reality testing or of communicating to others those self-deceiving activities that we see in them. Fortunately, the process of self-emancipation, once it begins, is highly gratifying and has its own built-in rewards.

This book views perception from an evolutionary perspective, among others. Our Stone Age ancestors had to assume that what they encountered was reality, for there it was in earth and stone, in blood and bone. Then, with instruments like Archimedes' lens and Galileo's telescope, they learned that there was more out there that had never been seen or guessed. The structure of modern science has risen largely from new devices for apprehending what was hidden. Man finds that he is being threatened or destroyed by that which he has neither observed with the naked eye nor suspected existed —viruses, for example, or the first beginnings of malignant growth—and he bends every energy to extend his grasp, to pull into clear observation that which lies unseen.

Yet we continue to assume, as a rule, that the unknown is essentially similar to what we have always known. In the early maps of Columbus's era, sea serpents often looked like serpents already known, and when men of other regions were encountered, they were assumed to be like Robinson Crusoe's Man Friday, endowed with the same attributes of head, heart, and body familiar to navigators. Even today, light may be described as quanta or as waves, but it does not occur to us that it might be virtually an infinity of *other* things. The new must be perceived in terms of the familiar, and even when we know this, we still are bound to assume, as we extend our contact with reality, that what we discover will be more real things and real processes that are *like* the ones we already know.

The thesis of this essay is that humankind has very curiously

and subtly, very ingeniously and systematically, prevented itself from reaching out to new types of reality. This is partly
because we defend ourselves against a bolder type of extension
of knowledge. We shall argue that man is forever at work keeping vast areas of unwelcome reality out of his view, trying
especially to suppress knowledge of his own nature. Charles
Darwin was aware of this tendency, and in the record he kept
of all biological evidence that bore on his theory of evolution,
he made it a rule to note in particular the bits of evidence that
told *against* his theory. The cases that told in favor of his
theory he knew he would be more likely to remember.

Finally, is it *possible* to see the world totally without bias?
This is another question that this book tries to open up for
discussion.

I learned much about self-deception from Eugen Bleuler's
insights into autistic thinking and from the studies of the influence of drive upon perception, memory, and thought,
which flourished under Harry A. Murray at the Harvard
Psychological Clinic in the thirties. I was privileged to find
at the City College of New York in the early forties a group
of collaborators in the form of honors students of psychology,
notably Robert Levine, Roy Schafer, Harold Proshansky,
Leo Postman, and Jerome Levine. From 1952 onwards, I
was able to continue such studies at The Menninger Foundation in Topeka, Kansas, with the help of a group of collaborators, including Robert Sommer, Harold McNamara,
Ralph Fisch, Fred and Charles Snyder, John Santos, Bobby
Farrow, and especially Charles M. Solley, whose integration
of these studies along the way led to the volume: Solley and
Murphy, *Development of the Perceptual World*, 1960. This
served as a recapitulation and prospectus of research on the
dynamics of cognition and perception. Solley did much to
straighten and tighten up my thinking. But as the reader will
see, that thinking is not completed, and perhaps its lack of
completion will keep the system of ideas open for new ideas
and new experiments. Herbert Spohn helped me clarify my

ideas (Murphy and Spohn, *Encounter with Reality*, 1968).
While unable to agree with Eleanor J. Gibson, I have learned
much from her. The National Institute of Mental Health supported many of the studies mentioned in Chapter 5.

The system of ideas presented here is quite different from
my earlier work. I have incorporated the development of
feedback theory and the conception that the whole process of
perceiving is in some respects self-correcting through the ad-
justment of acts of perceiving resulting from new activity
that the perceiving organism carries out as new bursts of information are received. My current ideas, not basically in
contrast with those of Dewey and Bentley on "transactional
psychology," nor of Piaget on the subject of "assimilation"
and "accommodation," are a part of a general modern movement toward the recognition of feedback principles in the
life sciences.

The material tapped is heavily experimental but is not
purely from the field of perception or even psychology.
Rather, psychological and physiological experiments and insights are drawn upon, ranging through a broad spectrum of
research. In the later pages, biographical materials are used for
contrast and example, since for many readers these reach
home more quickly than experimental materials.

A final note. As far as the mechanics of writing are concerned, the "I" referred to itinerantly is Gardner Murphy,
who wrote the manuscript. Morton Leeds edited and revised
the basic materials somewhat and provided many of the mechanical aids that make it easier to read and use.

Outgrowing
Self-Deception

CHAPTER 1

The Too-Muchness
of Reality

In the course of evolution, living things have had to be able to make sense of their environment. They have had to adapt to food, danger, and each other. They have had to develop increasingly proficient sense organs for adaptively selecting, from all the hurly-burly about them, the few things that are relevant to their lives. The chick selects the dark object moving overhead and scurries for cover. The woodtick hangs on a high branch until a hog passes beneath, smelling of butyric acid. He drops, he lands, he burrows in. In this way animals learn to use their senses functionally, in terms of an ongoing activity or purpose at a given time.

For the most part, sense organs have developed because they make adaptation possible, and the ways in which action patterns follow from the arrival of messages suggest that the best action patterns are instigated by sense messages. Yet mistakes, and grievous ones, do occur. When a scarlet tanager flies against a picture window, one realizes that the world of "illusions" belongs not only to mankind but also to beast and bird. The arts of the fisherman and trapper, successful through all of human history, testify to the "misinterpretations," the nonadaptive responses, that living things make to their environment.

THE NEED FOR BLINDERS

When it comes to human response to this enigmatic world, the opportunities for self-deception (or inappropriate response to signals) are grossly multiplied. Indeed, we shall see that the too-muchness of life requires, from the viewpoint of society, that young and old acquire blinders as well as selectors lest the overload be unbearable; lest we make dangerous misinterpretations—dangerous to the individual or to the group—and lest threats multiply beyond all possibility of our successfully confronting them.

The little beast or bird must have a primitive reliance on its capacity to meet the endless cycle of threats. It must not stand timidly by or practice the "death feint" continuously. It must have what George Santayana calls "animal faith": one must push along with the day's excitements. We have seen tiny fishes play about the nose of a half-grown alligator. Occasionally, one is snapped up, but the rule is to ignore the threatening teeth. In the long run, individual adaptation is not perfect. It is the group that must survive.

At the human level there must be a firm conviction that one sees the world as it really is. The philosopher's doubts must not interfere with the first enormous delight of being a little child exploring the world. But living things must not only accept the real; being imperfectly adapted to all of reality, they must also accept much of the not-real as real. They must at times be self-deceived. In essence, the first need of the young is to believe in themselves and act on this belief, even when it is not wholly sound.

Society must allow the young their blinders. However, the blinders are often too crude to serve their purpose well. They lack subtlety. They lack individuation. So we also need various kinds of lenses. We need magnifying glasses through which we can emphasize what seems good and, as we shall see, we need reversed opera glasses to reduce the size of a threat or a blow. We must accept the distortions that our needs require; we must accept the lenses that reduce the problems we cannot solve.

Our blinders maintain not only our self-images but also our images of our family and friends. Everyone who is precious to us receives the side benefits of some idealization or exaggerated gifts of charm, wit, insight, or strength. We don't quite admit that they have great weaknesses as well, and perish the thought that any of them are plain ordinary folks.

As parents, we think our children's teachers are stupid and insensitive not to realize the unusual talent—latent, to be sure, but great—in our young ones. "If my boy isn't doing well in school, there is something wrong with the school," says the adoring mother, blind to the short attention span of her restless son.

Our parents, if not brilliant, are resourceful, courageous, or unique in some way; their prejudices in our favor require us to maintain the blinders that prevent us from seeing their insensitivity or callousness to the needs of others. Our own uniqueness came to us naturally, of course, from such unusual parents.

But blinders can also work negatively: when we have to defend a permanent lawsuit, as it were, against parents or siblings against whom we carry a lifelong grudge. He was stingy (and we don't recognize that he was struggling with severe financial limitations). Or he was not at all perceptive (perhaps because he was preoccupied with a complicated invention that required concentrated work). The blinders may shut out a wide range of possibilities. (Sometimes all the members of the opposite sex are rejected.) In politics, many Democrats dismiss all Republicans with the blind conviction that Republicans don't care about people while the Republicans dismiss Democrats as socialists or soft, permissive, or unrealistic.

In these and other instances, blinders shut out evidence that would contribute to a balanced and objective view of the person or group that we defend (as an extension of ourselves) or reject (as dangerous or hateful). In clinical work we use terms like "denial," "repression," and "projection" to describe the processes by which the blinders are maintained. David Hamburg has shown how some people dying of very severe burns managed to cope with the desperate situation by insisting that they were recovering. Children often insist that they "cannot" succeed with a certain task while all the time they are studying the problems involved so that they can develop an inner plan for mastering it.

When blinders are maintained by repression of unbearable aspects of reality, however, they may shut out potentially helpful experiences as well. "I have had two lives and I have to forget the first one," said a twelve-year-old who deeply resented his natural father's hostility to his mother and stepfather. In the process of repressing the bitter thoughts, he repressed the many good contributions his father had made to his earliest years.

Perhaps most destructive are the blinders that shut out all awareness of those aspects of our "enemy" that might make it possible to resolve conflicts without so much bloodshed, so much despoiling of land and property. Once named as enemy, only those facts and fictions that support the image are allowed. When the battle is over, the "enemy" quality may vanish, as with Japan and West Germany, and friendship, even admiration, may flow once more.

We may keep blinders on to prevent ourselves from fully realizing potential capacities: we refuse to dare a difficult challenge lest we fail. Realizing that others may expect too much, we play down our real abilities just to learn a margin for safe progress. This is the pattern of many an "underachiever" who refuses to work "up to capacity" as his capacity is seen by his teachers. Of course, many a youth today consciously rejects the "rat race" because he sees through the deceptions inherent in intense competition. But unconsciously he may feel that he cannot top the achievements of his father and it is safer not to try.

In other words, blinders may be used to defend success and prestige or to defend against getting trapped by the drive to achieve. Blinders may protect against fears, dangers, or threats of many kinds—whether threats to physical survival (as with the people who live along the San Andreas fault, where an earthquake is bound to occur), to lovableness, to financial security (as with gamblers who cannot be objective about chances of loss), or to health (as with smokers who believe that cancer "won't happen to me").

THE AUTOKINETIC EFFECT

The matter of perceiving as we need to perceive can be pushed much further. Take an experiment carried out by Bobby Farrow with the "autokinetic effect." This relates to a stationary point of light in a jet-black dark room. The light, for most observers, appears to move about. Both the amount and direction of movement depend not only on the point of light and the darkness but also on the personality of the observer and the attitude he takes toward the task. Farrow measured the autokinetic effect for each of his subjects: how far the light moved for each one. But he did more. From time to time the experimenters caused the light to move: it *really* moved. When the light shone at certain points—in certain quadrants of the whole visual field—the subject received a painful electric shock. When the light appeared in *other* quadrants, no shock was given. Before long, the subject had acquired a strong tendency to *see the light only in quadrants that had not been "punished"* by the shock. The light, so to speak, "learned" to keep away from dangerous areas; the light "behaved" and kept one out of the danger zone!

Perceptual distortion can be demonstrated by an experimenter's "trick," but it is a constant of life experience. And where a whole group has shared an experience, they see differently than do other groups. Some preliterate tribes, for instance, can see a ladder standing upright, but they literally cannot see it at all when it is on the ground. We shut out what we do not want to see by drooping eyelids or squinting or turning away or by the half dozen other tricks described in Chapter 5.

SCREENING IN AND SCREENING OUT

The approach to reality works as a unit, and so likewise does the system of avoidance of reality. It has essentially the same central purpose: adaptation to the environment. But there are modes of adaptation that are too simple to be effective in man's socially competitive world of loves and hates, aspirations and disappointments. Here we must learn to screen in and screen out with equal skill.

Basically, we have two ways of ordering reality: the way of science and the way of personal desires. We need experience and skill in order to find objective relevance in most of the distant events of a chaotic world before we succumb to seeing them in terms of our personal needs. For the most part, one chooses a good blend of the two, including, as a kind of middle ground, perception in terms of the needs of other members of the community.

Personal styles in encountering reality and in escaping reality make up much of the world of history, contemporary biography, and politics. The ways of knowing, the "cognitive styles" so ingeniously investigated in the last few years, appear to be mainly styles of avoiding, blocking, or inhibiting all unwelcome information, or on the other hand, styles of combining, enriching, and fortifying the channels that bring us what we want. Personal styles of encounter and escape, like almost everything in human nature, probably have a "hereditary component." But they also reflect previous experience, or as with the tea taster or the well-trained musician, they owe much to training in the use of the senses. So the task of clearly perceiving depends on both *selecting* and *enriching* that which the senses bring us. Full confrontation with the world—and the reduction of error in the process—depends partly on learning to use the senses and partly on learning not to use them.

We have greatly varying individual capacities for receiving or rejecting the messages that continually come to us. "Cognitive bias" describes the combination of hereditary and experiential conditions that exist prior to these messages. In confronting our environment, we learn to exploit whatever abilities we have. The effect of equal training has been found to increase, rather than reduce this individuality. When we see children of school age or in early adolescence coming to terms with tests, we find each individual learning to enhance whatever capacities and whatever cognitive bias he already has. The principle, as Thorndike said, is, as a rule, not compensation, but correlation; not "evening up," but "to him that hath shall be given." The result is that self-deception in some individuals tends to increase, whereas others learn to cultivate the very fine art of seeing the things that others do not see as well—or at all.

CHAPTER 2

―――

The Joy of the Real

Poetry belongs to real things, and to real things only.
—Walt Whitman

PROPHETS AND PHILOSOPHERS have often warned people against overreliance on their senses. But the senses do have "work" to do, and even when they are "off duty" they offer us some of life's greatest delights.

Especially in childhood, the senses can be sources of enormous joy. The "sensory toys" of L. J. Stone and L. B. Murphy included velvet and sandpaper, cold cream and fingerpaints, for preschoolers to rub through their fingers with an explorer's yen and an artist's sensitivity. Fingerpaints and brush paints yield beautiful creations in the hands of four-year-olds who immerse themselves in the joy of the sensory world and in the joy of the muscular action of manipulating and combining the sensory stuff. They learn to intensify these delights by differentiating among touches and colors and by combining them, both randomly and in an ordered, original way.

When taste and smell are involved, as with professional tea and wine tasters, one begins to see the basis of a primary human capacity for combating self-deception—namely, the rich pleasure that is originally associated with the tea or wine itself comes to be associated with the process of differentiating. The gourmet may extend his skill to a very broad range of qualities in foods and drinks, as the perfumer may extend it to a very wide array of olfactory delights. George Santayana thinks of philosophers as specializing in different smells. The charming French philosopher Condillac (1754) asks us to imagine a statue with the sense of smell, and from this sense of smell, deriving in time all the modalities of human experience —sensory, cognitive, and affective. Thousands of delightful odor and taste patterns involving touch and temperature factors from the tongue, mouth, and nasal membranes (and action patterns, too, as in sniffing, inhaling, or swallowing), make these "simpler senses" far from simple. At a still higher level, the full range of a musician's delights in comparing the tone of an old spinet or harpsichord with the earliest of modern pianos, or the pleasure a lover of Turner may enjoy in comparing the various ochers, oils, and water-color combinations, may give us a first glimpse into the riches of this very process of reality confrontation.

ARE THE SENSES "DECEIVERS"?

We are living creatures in contact with a warmly fulfilling environment; our sensory experiences are rooted at least in a very rich psychological reality, whether or not they are the ultimate reality of the philosopher's quest. There is a kind of reality that neither science nor philosophy can describe: for example, the kinds of experiences arising in our inner world as we confront a red, red rose or a balsam pillow. The psychology of the senses begins just beyond the point where physical science has to stop. There are, indeed, dimensions according to which olfactory elements can be arranged, but the thousands of terms used for the whole range of olfactory and gustatory delight refers to personal realities, some of them shared and some of them unique.

We use these illustrations rather than the familiar illustrations from sight and hearing (so consistently chosen by philosophers in relation to the problem of the real) because we want to make the most of the fact that there is, from infancy onward, an intense human impulsion toward the real, constantly appearing on the borderline between the "subjective world" and the world described by the physical sciences. Indeed it is this manifestly real world that stands out with such enormous value and importance in the experience of the small child—the world of tastes, touches, colors, burns, aches, the world of muscular tension under drowsiness and under alertness. These sensory experiences not only have the philosophical virtue of being primary "reals" for the child; they have the further value, so essential in our present quest, of showing that the love of sensory experience may draw us away from all self-deception.

PERSONAL REALITY

As an experience becomes more complex, as we pass from a single tone to a Beethoven symphony or from a dab of color to a Venetian sunset, we often lose ourselves not in "illusion" but in a personal "reality." Through analyzing the sensory manifold, observing the differentiated details, and then making higher units or organized forms or patterns out of the totality, we achieve a stable structure, a perceptual whole. The conquest of reality is paralleled by increasing intensities of sensory joy. In Henry T. Moore's experiment, simple chords repeated over and over again become monotonous, while complex tone patterns at first involving unacceptable relationships like diminished sevenths become, through long listening, more and more agreeable. The seeking of reality is partly the joy of elementary sense qualities and partly the experience of "progressive mastery." The real world arrives in the sheer process of becoming human, of growing up human. It can be weakened by attacks upon the sensory life, or by denial of the possibility that we *can* perceive reality from such elemental human experience. But if there is no such ax to grind, one of the most powerful of all human drives toward reality is the sheer drive to make the most of sensory experience, both in its simple and in its derivative forms.

However, in sensory pleasures there is much more than the sheer differentiation and integration of sensory values. There are also dozens—or thousands—of associations between the sensory material of the moment and other patterns of sensory experience coming from memories of other times and places—as, for example, in comparing one magnificent symphony with another, or the bouquet of one wine with that of another. This was illustrated charmingly a few years ago when a study was made of the great appeal of Mogen David wine. It turned out not to be the appearance, taste, smell, or any other simple sensory value or combination of values, but the "family quality" or "home quality" that was successfully emphasized in advertising; and it was not just a "Jewish wine" but also a wine very widely loved by nearly all members of the area studied. This quality of belonging to home and family is probably no more complex than most of the multiple values that appear even with simple sensory gratifications, as when the simple hearing of the first line of a lovely sonnet— "When to the sessions of sweet silent thought"—calls to mind the subsequent evocation of reality-rooted needs and gratifications.

THE DELIGHT OF DIFFERENTIATION

The activity of comparing and contrasting sense impressions is an additional satisfaction. The senses seem to follow the rule that organisms enjoy the normal utilization of all their equipment, if free of gross conflict or the arousal of punishments or pain associated with the utilization of organic equipment as such. Children learn to differentiate sense impressions partly through the delight in making these differentiations and partly through the secondary delight of being rewarded for the differentiation successfully made. Recent work has shown that the tiny infant confronting a patterned or structured field will look at it for much longer periods than at homogeneous fields. There is an interesting job to be done; there is more appeal in stimuli that permit active differentiation.

Human beings tend to push these differentiations as far as they can be pushed. Each individual makes visual or tactual differentiations as precisely as his organic equipment allows, but there is also a practice factor, as in learning to read Braille. P. O. Makarov asked the interesting question: Can we study in the *interior* of the body the same capacity for differentiation between points of stimulation that we can carry out on the skin? Of course, we have on our fingertips (and the tip of our tongue) very refined capacities to tell whether we are being stimulated at one or at two points at a given time. But suppose we ask how far the inner stimulation of the mucous membranes of the stomach can be pushed? Suppose we use tiny electric stimulators, swallowed and positioned to allow observations of the interior of the stomach? Makarov found that differentiation could be made only when two points were several centimeters apart. Our first thought here might be that this is the human "physiological limit," depending upon the sheer arrangement of the sense organs on the stomach surface. But another possibility occurs to us: Could it be that these differentiations are seldom (if ever) *practiced* so as to reveal their limits? In the case of the "two-point threshold" of the skin, we expect our limits to depend upon the anatomical closeness of the delicate little sense organs, yet some differentiation related to practice has regularly been found. It is therefore quite possible that the *internal* world is also quite capable of very much finer differentiation after prolonged and motivated practice.

FEELINGS ABOUT THE SELF

This, incidentally, has some bearing upon our general theme of self-deception. Perhaps the massive feelings that we have regarding our state of well-being may vary moment by moment, as a result of messages from the interior of our bodies, and the bodily messages may be very poorly distinguished. We may then begin to feel better, but if we have a hypochondriac conviction that we "feel lousy," we may cling to the bad feeling. So, too, our feelings about people may get "stuck" at a given level, and our judgments of music or literature may remain "stuck," simply because we have never trained ourselves to notice small, though real, differences. A man who knows his wine can easily satisfy other wine connoisseurs that no champagne can ever be an *Asti Spumanti*, and yet we may never succeed in teaching him that every Rembrandt is different from every Rubens. It is partly, of course, a question of visual differentiation, but it is also a question of subtle, yet massive, feelings that the one can stir up but the other cannot. We are slow and inept in learning to recognize such feelings unless we specifically undertake to train ourselves along these lines. Our feelings, especially about ourselves as persons of worth, are often massive, cloudlike, and inarticulate; we may be inclined to love or hate ourselves. We are seldom much motivated to make refined differentiations as we would in comparing people of complex personalities and varying worth about whom we must make refined judgments. It is quite possible that very massive differentiations between joy and agony are all that we really want to make in relation to our feelings about our own worth, especially our worth as judges of things beautiful and noble. We may have to admit that our nose is snub or flat or hawklike, but which of our internal qualities can be precisely defined and judged in this way? Self-deception about inner qualities occurs directly because of the blur, the crudity, of inner observation.

PROGRESSIVE MASTERY

There is surely plenty of evidence that making differentiations can at times be highly agreeable, and that the discovery of differences involves the novelty factor, the progressive-mastery factor, and the exhilaration of using our equipment in a new way. In countercamouflage—as when one sees through a disguise and detects a ship's contours even in the cleverly portrayed lines of harbor, fortress, and coastal shrubbery—the misleading cues may suddenly be detected and "seen through." A sudden flash of understanding or of humor may come as one catches the point of a mystifying sophistry; or the awful but inevitable solution to a well-hidden "mystery" allows us to put together suddenly a variety of clues. In Arthur Koestler's *The Act of Creation*, we suddenly see how to apply several ways of thinking to one concrete situation; there is often a sense of power, as when we watch our rival lose his balance; or delight in a clear achievement, as when Little Jack Horner encounters the plum; or emerging safety and self-assertion in the toddler's seeing what was hidden: "You play no tricks on me."

Perhaps the simplest everyday development of reality-oriented perception from a crude to a sophisticated level involves a little of all these factors. Take the simplest illustration of passage from noise to tone: one hears at a distance an unstable and meaningless sound, which as one approaches becomes first a rhythm and then a band playing, or a conversation between friends, with more and more differentiation, integration, meaning, and satisfaction at each step in one's progress. All of this constitutes progressive discovery of and rejoicing in reality. Whatever greater complexities come from education and psychotherapy, or from group exploratory effort, must at least use all these simpler reality-seeking factors.

But the senses do not always speak clearly to us. Everyday women and men as well as philosophers enjoy not merely seeing but seeing clearly. They dislike fog and smog. They like to hear the voices around them come through distinctly. In recent experiments, even monkeys have been found to prefer clear to indistinct pictures. Children like to rub their fingers along surfaces that have definite messages to offer: smooth things, flat things, or sharp edges. On the other hand, confused sounds, "dark-brown tastes," and all that is unclear annoy us. This is partly, no doubt, because these blurred signals afford only ambiguous cues for action. Just plain *listening*, however, as to a divertimento, or just plain *looking* on a cloudless and hazeless mountain range, can give peace and delight.

STRUCTURE

Often we seek *simple* structure, moving from complex figures to circles, triangles, rectangles. We have noted, however, many instances in which *complex* structure is highly gratifying. In the arts one progresses with delight from simple structure to the interplay of structure within a more complex whole; the composer "develops" a theme; the poet creates the rich melody of a Petrarchan sonnet. We should gravely miss the point if we were to insist that there is a universal tendency toward simplicity, as toward the simple circle by contrast with a Gothic cathedral or a bland, pure tone as contrasted with the resonant complexities of Tchaikovsky or Sibelius. Simplicity proves to be a factor that we need, but simple structure does not tell the whole story. To find order and simplicity in the world about us is not subjective or arbitrary. Rhythm, balance, order, structure are concepts imposed by the real balance, rhythm, and order of natural forces. Even in the complexities of progressive mastery, we follow an orderly path. One can experience in oneself the simultaneous delight of searching and finding a simple pattern, and the detachment of this pattern from a still more complex whole, as in the embedded figures test, below.

Find *A* in *B*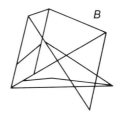

Figure 1. Embedded Figures Test.

CURIOSITY

By such devices as the embedded figure test, one may, while measuring the individual's capacity for discovering parts inherent in a whole, also illustrate the human delight in the kind of *activity* that is called into play by this test, by the urge to break the complexity into simple, manageable parts: the act of seeking, the "wrestling with the angel" to reveal his secrets. This, of course, is related to the love of novelty and the other aspects of curiosity, as shown, for example, in the work of D. E. Berlyne. In a far-flung experimental program, Berlyne showed the enormous motivating power of many factors in stimulating the cognitive activities that we lump together as "curiosity." Of special importance are *novelty* and *change*. We do not say that curiosity is a simple, easily identifiable drive; rather, that not only are the senses gratifying in their own right but the drive to immerse oneself in sensory qualities involves the drive to differentiate them, make the most of their variety, and, as we shall later see, integrate them so as to make a more understanding response to them.

One of the great curiosity researchers, Harry Harlow, tells the story of an infant, "Mary" who, if the word "drive" can *ever* be used in psychology, surely had a drive to perceive:

"When Mary X was held in any position depriving her of visual exploration of the environment, she screamed; when held in a position favorable to visual exploration of the important environment, which did not include the parent, she responded positively. With the parent and position held constant and visual exploration denied by snapping off the electric light, the positive responses changed to negative, and they returned to positive when the light was again restored." Like many other babies, she simply wanted to be able to *see*.

THE CONSTANCIES

We have ordinarily a strong inner set or preparedness to perceive as we have always perceived, and this set can lead to curious "illusions" and "misperceptions." We see the coal as black and the snow as white, although at a given time and place, much more light may be reflected from the former than from the latter. This phenomenon of "constancies" is, of course, highly relevant to our observations of ourselves. We are the selves that we "know"; we see ourselves in terms of constancies. We meet ourselves on the road or in the moment of pride or shame as the same old person that we thought we could count on. This may remind us of the need to have people "stay put," per our preconceptions.

It has been shown in experiments that if a man wears lenses to throw the world upside down, in time the upside-down world comes right side up again. It takes work, but it finally succeeds. There is, therefore, no surprise for us in the fact that seeing ourselves in our usual way has value because it is familiar, and a further value because we have, as Freud would say, "invested" in it. And the whole world is structured largely in relation to ourselves. When our behavior or that of the world is different from the ordinary response for which we are set, we may find ourselves annoyed or threatened. How we are bothered by acquaintances from long ago who don't look as they *should* look in terms of our memories regarding them! And it is worse if they were close friends with whom there is an experience not only of shock but also of their failure to live up to the benign image of them that we have done so much to cultivate.

Finally, we have abundant experimental evidence that we can learn to see things as they assuredly are not. In the Princeton laboratory, F. L. Kilpatrick introduced his subjects to a series of little "rooms." Looking through a peephole into the first, one sees a well-shaped hollow cube with floor and ceiling perpendicular to the sides, as in an ordinary room.

Figure 2. Inverted Truncated Pyramid.

Then one tosses a ball, which bounces so peculiarly that one soon begins to grasp that the room is not a cube at all but a truncated inverted pyramid. Within thirty or forty minutes the room comes to be seen as what it really is (see Figure 2).

The cubical relationships have given way to the true perception of the inverted pyramid. Then the subject is wheeled about and looks through a peephole into a second room. He sees it as a truncated inverted pyramid. Actually it is nothing of the sort; it is a true cube! First he learned to see the room as it is; now he sees it as it is not. The point at issue is whether the practice in seeing always leads to correctness of seeing, and the answer is no.

Similar evidence is offered in an experiment performed in the Menninger laboratory by H. J. McNamara, who rewarded certain subjects for seeing and reporting lines longer than they were, thereby producing in his subjects a generalized tendency to overestimate line length. Other subjects were rewarded for underestimating line length and learned just as well to "see short." Then when he shifted his subjects from horizontal to vertical lines, and from one numerical system of gauging the distance to another system, the training carried over to the new situation; the overestimating subjects went on overestimating, and the underestimating subjects went on underestimating. It is hard to support the view that more and more sheer exposure to reality necessarily improves coping with it. It depends on the consequences of the exposure.

Psychologists have listened to a controversy in recent years regarding how our first raw experiences are elaborated as the process of perceptual learning goes forward. One viewpoint is that new associative links are formed. The world of association supplements the world of sensory impact. Another view is that there is no need for such associative operation: there is only the need for taking in what is already there; there must simply be a process of enrichment. Surely, there can be a great deal of enrichment, and at the same time plenty of room for fresh associations and for an abundance of memories, called out in unique fashion for different people at different times.

But a legitimate emphasis here is on the drive to learn, the urge to acquire perceptual skills. It does not take an external reward to get the individual to move toward more elaborate and more satisfying patterns of sensory differentiation and integration. From the very beginning, as we saw, there is an urge toward structure rather than emptiness, blur, or chaos. There are further delights in stability as contrasted with instability of the end product. The situation is strongly loaded in favor of the organism's responding to the simple, to the new, to the changing, and finally, after the task is done, to the firmly structured.

The self, too, is perceived in structured wholeness in this way. But we must remember that this is not necessarily the way the self really is. We have learned from experimental studies that there is a great deal in life that structures an unrealistic picture of the self and in this particular area the dice are heavily loaded against one's understanding what has been going on.

THE SEEKING OF GOOD FORM

Perception involves interpretation of form. Rudolf Arnheim has shown the interplay of various kinds of form in a structured representation of the external world, through the pictorial arts and through sculpture and through architecture. Lancelot Whyte has drawn together observations from geometry, astronomy, genetics, zoology, and psychology showing the role of the mathematically simple, the perceptually clear, in making the world satisfying and manageable.

Moreover, we tend mostly to see that which has good form, whether the form corresponds to some empirical reality or not. We try to remove complexities; we seek, as the Gestalt psychologist would say, good form. The principle of goodness may keep reappearing at higher levels. But this is not *always* true. And it would be paradoxical to give a roundworm or even an amoeba a higher evolutionary position than a primate because of the relative simplicity, the regularity, the orderliness of its form. It would likewise be paradoxical to assume that a low-grade mental defective, because he is simple and good, is in any sense at a higher level, or represents the principle of goodness more adequately, than a person of organized intellect and personality.

We may safely say that percepts tend toward lawful form, and that in some cases there is much *delight in simplification*; this is indeed a basic principle for the theory of self-deception. We want things simple; we need things simple, both for the obvious reasons already mentioned and because over-simplification is often an escape from the reality of our inadequacies.

In discussions like these, one is often told that the real issue is "relevance" or "meaning." One finds meaning in one's environment. It has relevance. Psychologists prefer to say that the world tends to be seen in terms of our total adaptive needs. The seriousness of this conclusion for the problem of man's basic self-deception is inadequately realized by pragmatists, relationists, and all who feel that self-deception is a minor, secondary problem in man's struggle to cope with the world and its dangers. The conclusion is not pessimistic, but it is sober and somber. It suggests that we need much more radical devices for learning to see man as he is and learning to see ourselves as we are.

But the re-educational possibilities, instead of being grim duties, can be matters of profound gratification. (1) They start with the delight in sheer sensory contact with reality; (2) they go on through the world of learning to perceive, to make differentiations and integrations, and to achieve more complex stable structures; (3) then they involve the satisfaction of seeing oneself in a meaningful relation to a complex and orderly world; and (4) they offer the possibility that the sheer use of one's mind in doing all this can be a gratifying experience.

CHAPTER 3

―――

The Emergence of
Self-Awareness

―――

Let us recapitulate and expand the ideas presented so far: the world of sensory stimulation is not only a source of information but also, inherently and directly, a source of gratification—gratification so great that it can become effective in reducing the errors in perceiving (and in thinking) to which we are subject. Not a moralistic demand upon ourselves to be "honest" and to "face reality," but a positive cultivation of delight in the exploratory approach to the world, may effectively reduce the escapist, "autistic," or wish-fulfilling dangers to which we are prone by virtue of both evolutionary and cultural pressures.

But let us look at all this in a somewhat broader context. There is not much reason to believe that the newborn infant is aware of himself. There is no way of knowing very accurately whether his world really is, as William James said, a "blooming, buzzing confusion." At times there is evidence, however, of a certain thunderous tumult, a certain diffuse sensitivity and vulnerability, in which hands and feet, head, speech equipment, and vital organs all seem to be saying something that is very far from being nicely differentiated into the functioning parts that we think of as characterizing a well-structured personality. The little infant interferes with his own ongoing activity, not seeming to know what is wrong. As with the "split-brained" monkey, one of whose hands obstructs what the other has been trained to do, one habit system can interfere with another, and the thoughtful observer is likely to conclude that there really are rather independent functioning systems at work. Indeed, there are probably, from moment to moment, many such functioning systems. This is to be expected when one considers the complexity of the body and the complexity of the world, which have to be brought into relation one with another: the multitude and complexity of the signals have to be hooked to specific interactions with the environment. Thus, the systematic investigators of the modern era give us a picture of differentiation and integration that are achieved slowly, and with much struggle, by all normal infants.

The very last thing we would expect a child to master is an awareness of his own totality as a person, and this, indeed, is achieved only slowly. For at any given level, or in any given situation, there are always parts of the bodily system, parts of the inner vital activity, parts of the symbol system, that are incompletely integrated, or temporarily in conflict. The symbol systems make up a considerable part of what is called the preconscious system in psychoanalytic terminology. Sometimes, they make up that pattern of conscious, preconscious, and unconscious components which psychoanalysts call the ego—that system of activities relating to one's own body and mind, one's loves and hates, control mechanisms, ways of remembering, fantasying, planning, and symbolizing.

The reason for recalling these points here is the fact that the capacity to deceive oneself and then, in some degree, to liberate oneself from such self-deception involves not only a process of confronting the outer world, but slowly and with difficulty facing and integrating one's impressions about his own *inner world,* as well. The newborn infant's awareness of the world or of himself and his actions is not clear enough to allow him to select from and organize outer with inner impressions. The ego is a control system, a way of saying yes to some impressions, no to others. It is a system of readiness, of low thresholds for the admission or exclusion of messages, and, consequently, of schematic roles to be accepted and lived by, or to be whisked away, or trampled on. It is related, indeed, to habits of attention, and to the drives associated with each relevant stimulus calling for approach, denial, or escape; one child approaches what another escapes.

DIFFERENTIATION OF THE MOTHER AND THE SELF

Infants can learn only from experience. Babies have very different opportunities for observing and exploring. Summer babies in warm parts of the United States are often dressed in nothing but a diaper. They can see their arms, legs and abdomens. By contrast, winter babies, protected by coveralls, are prevented from seeing anything but their hands; consequently, they are not able to connect visual observations with kinesthetic and tactile sensations. Similarly, a Nigerian baby, strapped to his mother's back and carried about as she goes on her errands, observes much of the world in passing, but he cannot see any part of himself and can see only his mother's back. Such differences in recurrent experiences have important implications for the development of the baby's awareness of himself as a whole, as well as his awareness of his mother.

The white middle-class American baby who is left in a crib for much of the day, with recurrent experiences of being picked up and put back into the crib, has typical sequences of isolation and together-with-mother experiences. The separations provide a foundation for a sense of self-alone which many babies protest. By contrast, the baby in India who spends most of the day on his mother's hip or in a sling under her sari is experiencing sensations of union with mother. Such differences are important for the development (or lack of development) of a clear sense of an independent self and the differentiation of mother from other people. Touch, voice, ways of moving are all involved, but what the baby sees can tie these together. With the many variations in opportunities for sensory experience, it is not surprising that wide differences in the pace of these differentiations are found among different babies. Some babies as young as twelve weeks are frightened by a strange woman, while many others do not recognize a stranger until the age of six or eight months.

The sense of the self undoubtedly involves more than distal sensory experiences; babies influence the environment by protest, by pushing unwanted food out of the mouth or pushing unwanted objects away, by reaching toward and grasping or banging small objects, by innumerable contacts and impacts. All of these provide the baby with knowledge of the environment and what can be done with it. Infants who act on the environment in their early months develop more confidence and awareness of their own powers by the age of four or five. Still, a full sense of one's self and control over oneself may not appear until some years later.

THE ARTFUL DODGER

In his fantastic capacity to see the seamy side of life, half-hidden, half-blended into the endearing, tender world of love, respect, and pride, in the world of very plain people living very plain family lives, Charles Dickens introduces us to a young man of extraordinary capacities. He earns from his family and his boon companions the epithet "The Artful Dodger": he is capable of slipping past and away from, every comeuppance. We think of him here because dodging is one of the primary tasks involved in effective contact with a precarious and unorganized world; escaping, slipping away, filtering out through the interstices into the vast unknown in which most people would be lost—slipping, one might say, into the night. But the observant eye of Charles Dickens noticed also that this is not like the casual retreat from the world that takes place as we become bored or fatigued, or too sick or beaten to maintain contact. On the contrary, the process is highly "artful." It is a *skill*, a skill acquired over a long time and with much wit and effort. The selection of efficient ways of avoiding the outer world—and also the world within—is not one of those simple, inevitable, universal, and adaptive acts with which we are endowed by our sheer human nature. Rather it is a system of skills learned in different ways in different cultures, and by different techniques; learned by individuals, depending on their needs, their adaptive capacities, and the situations into which life has plunged them.

To think of avoidance as a skill becomes easier when we observe how small children in their paintings "filter" the meaningful things to be represented while rejecting the rest. Perceptual and motor skills develop together; the problem is partly one of perceptual filtering and partly one of capacity to execute on paper or in clay or mud what has been apprehended. The Goodenough test (in which a child is asked to draw a man) shows, for children of our industrialized society, the ways in which the body, the clothing, and the accepted form of posture, stance, locomotion are represented in such a way as to reveal to us how far they have gone toward breaking down and reorganizing their perceptual world in a way defined by our cultural refinements. While children of some American Indian tribes lag behind our own norms in this capacity to "draw a man," they have been shown to succeed admirably, ahead of our norms, in a "draw-a-horse" test.

THE SPIDER OF SELF

Such studies suggest that the growth of perception, in a highly organized and selective form, reflects the cultural requirements impressed upon the child, that it is expressive of the way in which family and society direct the development of an outlook upon world and self. It is not the sense organs, or even the modes of basic perceptual organization, that provide our main clues here. It is the dawning patterns of self-awareness that establish the basic ground rules of what is relevant or irrelevant and how to relate to the self all that has any specific meaning. The world is given a self-referencing treatment before it is ever allowed to get itself organized objectively. The individual is forever ordering the world in terms of himself. He is like the spider at the center of the web. Where else could the spider be than at the center of "reality"?

This is partly because the perception of the self—that is, of the total individual, including anatomy, physiology, memories, goals, and everything that goes with the individual package—is the one thing that is forever there; the self is perceived in all its demanding, threatening, permitting, promising aspects. Each life situation is one of the factors, along with many organic and life history factors, that make for uniqueness in the response to all such situations. In this figure-ground organization, the self may at times be figure, at times ground, but it is always present.

There is more, however, than the simple capacity for figure-ground structuring to give the self its predominance. The self is the center of *values*. As Paul Schilder admirably showed, the self is "cathected"; it is our major "investment." The individual, through his primitive joys and miseries, must come to be forever preoccupied, and at every level, with that which happens to the self. There is a type of suggestion sometimes used by hypnotists that says: "You will ex-

[29]

perience severe pain, and yet it will not really be *your* pain, and you won't mind." The self, this conglomerate pattern of personal individuality, is intimately tied to the most enduring of pleasures and pains, and self-deception is first and last a system of devices for enhancing and protecting this empirical self and for defending it against injury and calamity.

"SELF-REGARDING SENTIMENT"

The relation of self in this sense to the values and the enduring character of the individual was masterfully worked out by William McDougall. A sentiment, in McDougall's use, is a cluster of instinctive impulses invested in, or preoccupied with, a specific object. There are sentiments relating to family, home, neighborhood, country, and religion, to our uniquely personal value systems and the objects and symbols that stand for them, all organized as the structure of concerns that relate to the self. It is this firm sentiment oriented in and around the self which represents the structural core and the continuity of personal existence.

So, we say, there is not only great strength in this structural organization related to a deep reality; there is also a profound need to keep the structure stable, orderly, continuous, and dependable. In other words, seeing ourselves as we *need* to see ourselves, including the basic need for self-deception, is built in with the same firm stroke as is the reality factor. Men of firm character, men who can make decisions and act on them, are considered to have a "strong will." Men with weak or disorganized values, values not directly related to the self, or values that are embodied in conflictful aspects of the self are men with a "weak will." If there is poor material to work with, as in low-grade mental defects, behavior may lack control and be "impulsive"; but "character disorders" exist as well among those who have normal and above-normal intelligence and only fleeting and evanescent pictures of the self, or self-pictures that have not been worked through in relation to specific and accepted obligations in life. Or if, in illness or confusion, our self-image lacks our usual sturdy components, and we act angrily or irrationally, our friends say we are not "ourselves" today; tomorrow we shall "come to ourselves." The self-deceptions of self-righteous, duty-bound inquisitors involve an investment in the self which means plenty of "will" organized around misperception of their actual nature, and of the relations between themselves and others.

If it is true, as we have tried to show, that all perception is "distorted" through our needs, it would seem to follow that perception of self is especially subject to such distortion. There is scarcely anything we need more than to see ourselves in terms of the worth, the values that we would like to conceive of ourselves as embodying.

As infants, we become aware of the systems and organs of our bodies and learn to recognize the sound of our own voice, and soon thereafter the name assigned to us. In childhood and adolescence, we learn the expectations and responsibilities that go with our own individuality. All that we aim to achieve becomes organized around this picture of the self, and all our most deeply meaningful activities are pursued, not for a momentary escape from a little pain, but for protection from the savage and unbearable injury which mutilation of the self-image would entail.

THE COMPLEXITY OF SELF-DECEPTION SKILLS

Again, note the enormous complexity of the skills involved in self-deception. We must see the implications of what is being said about us, grasp whether an insult is involved or just sheer banter, see the effect upon our reputation of a possible admission. We must emulate the adroit fencer, who in his riposte carries out with one motion the effective parrying of his antagonist's thrust and the delivery of his own thrust. It is still more complex than that, however. We are not only parrying and thrusting at a physical level; we are parrying symbols, even symbols removed by several stages from the original blow. And we are thrusting with symbols of great complexity against the symbol system of our antagonist. It is partly because of the complexity of the individual signal system that one's defense must be personally unique. But it is partly because of the richness of one's self-image that one must be ready at all times to foresee that the most *unlikely* thrust is likely; some of us are, in fact, potentially cultivators of paranoid suspicion. If such individuals do not prepare themselves for all kinds of attacks from all types of people, they will fall, in a prestige-minded community, into a world of individualized, personalized dangers.

Sir J. G. Fraser tells us of the priest at Nemi who stands guard continually, his blade ever ready to strike out against the hidden foe who will advance and slay him under his sacred tree. He cannot tell who the attacker will be, but because he knows that the attacker will come, there is never a moment of peace.

The little child learns very early what he must see and not see, especially the expressions of face or voice that could be too threatening. At first he shares with brother and sister the extraordinary urge to see, and then later not to see, the storm clouds in father's face or not to hear the threat in mother's voice. Then if the communications systems still work dangerously at home, he learns first to perceive, then not to perceive, what the community has to offer. He carries this far; he builds memory barricades against early emotional experience and has a "childhood amnesia" from which he can recover only under special circumstances and with great effort, if at all.

This appears especially clearly in individual perception of members of other groups. He learns, for example, that Orientals are inscrutable; he can look straight at the "impassive" faces and not see fear or humor or tenderness. These are attributes that he and his Caucasian world have agreed not to see. He cannot see much but solemnity in a German face, levity and volatility in a French face. So far does he push these self-blinding skills that in describing groups alien to himself, like the Germans and the French, he has only a few superficial phrases in his college notebook regarding the surging passions that their own literature and drama express to them. Furthermore, this blindness is a group achievement as well as an individual achievement. And one must be known to be a true member of his own "in-group," maintaining a solid wall of social isolation between his own group and others, which is essential to the continuous success which he craves in seeing the world as a "sound" person must.

CONSENSUAL VALIDATION

The senses work together in this matter, as in most matters. If one cannot see signs of trouble in the brow or the corners of the lips, one also cannot hear them in the strident or rumbling tones of a potentially threatening voice. This "consensual validation" works superbly: "If there had been anything mean in his voice, I would have seen it in his face." Continuous battle is thus maintained against the sharing of social insights. Totalitarians who capture their unprepared enemies are sometimes successful in obliterating a weary captive's memory by building up for him an organized pseudo world of relatives and homeland, which gradually replaces

[33]

real memories and real communication. When a pseudo identity built on false materials is to be constructed, there must be no cracks in the wall. As in the autokinetic studies, there must be no light from any source other than the one controlled by the experimenter. For the separated man, there must be no woman in the vague distance who could possibly remind him of "her." A French widow asked me in 1918 if I thought there was one good German anywhere, and she then leaped to prevent my suggestion that there could be.

Some blinding is stimulated by the system of which we are part. Thus the members of any "establishment"—Pentagon, State Department, White House staff, boards of education, industry—develop a credo, a system of beliefs or assumptions, often a myth, which shapes their thinking and works to shut out evidence contrary to their assumptions. An example is the industrialist, otherwise humane and kind, who said that "we couldn't make any profit if we tried to find new jobs for men displaced by machines." It is probable that the higher the office, the further away it is from firsthand evidence and the real experience of people. Establishments can therefore become intrinsically depersonalizing, and depersonalization thickens the blinders that develop in order to support self-interest.

CHAPTER 4

The Fine Art of
Self-Deception

Therefore, O Painter, look carefully what part is
most ill favored in your own person, and take
particular pains to correct it in your studies. For
if you are coarse, your figures will seem the
same and be void of charm; and it is the same
with any part that may be good or poor in yourself; it will be shown in some degree in your
figures.

—Leonardo da Vinci,
Notebooks

FROM THE USUAL everyday vantage point, it is assumed that
every individual is able to discover and utilize his environment and that if he sees with normal eyes, he sees it as it is.
How could there be any doubt about that? Indeed, he utilizes
every organ, every tissue, every cell, to maintain his perspective, to avoid error, to check up on what others say, to
show them wrong, and to maintain in court, in neighborhood,
and in family, that confident inner awareness of being *right*
which makes him a normal and acceptable member of society. If he goes about convinced that he is wrong, he will
either display neurotic forms of disquiet that would drive
everyone crazy, or maintain that type of isolation from the

community that would mark him as kooky or psychotic. According to the ground rules of the game of life, he must consider himself essentially right.

Moreover, on all essential matters that involve the life of the community, as against other communities, he learns to see that he has the pattern straight and that his whole group is right. The marble-playing boys of Neuchâtel, Switzerland, solemnly explained to Eugene Lerner that the boys of Geneva didn't really understand the game and played by the wrong rules; the Neuchâtel boys were similarly scorned by the Geneva boys. Whether it be men versus women, whites versus blacks, or Catholics versus Protestants, one shares one's rightness with a group of others who give support and collective assurance.

We can watch a child learn to do this, or rather, we can accurately see the precise skills that he acquires over a number of years in this process. Let us begin with his eyes. To take an elementary function first, when the world is threatening, he blinks; his eyes swing away from objects which must not be seen. Later he squints. Or he looks right through you without seeing you. At a higher level, the conjurer—or the politician—enables us to see what isn't there.

Many auditory signals are hard for us to detect. We hear perhaps two-thirds of what is said and fill in the rest, and later we and our interlocutors disagree as to what was really said. We know in a general way that "old people aren't as deaf as they seem," or we read in a solemn medical textbook that "paranoid delusions frequently appear in the deaf." Like the rest of us, they "imagine what they cannot hear." Or social isolation has become so painful that one must exaggerate it to make oneself pitiful or more conspicuous. Or one builds up a competing world of a "let's pretend" social character, which makes possible the defensive organization against those who would tell us that we are old or weak or unworthy of their attention.

Eyes and ears work pretty well together. Touch is a bit

harder to deceive. Macbeth, seeing a bloody dagger hanging in the air, shouts, "Here, let me clutch thee," and failing to make contact, says, "I have thee not." It works all too well with Lady Macbeth, who in the sleepwalking scene cannot even rub off the "damned spot" which clings to her murderous hand. Pains and aches are rather easily hallucinated; they serve a magnificent masking effect as secondary annoyances to keep our primary griefs from breaking into the chamber of consciousness. These delusions are not predominantly reflections of the external situation; they represent enormously intense cravings and dreads related to the self. Where sensory material is poorly structured, as is true in general of the world of smell, taste, touch, and temperature factors, we supply the structure ourselves. When perfume manufacturers and advertisers achieve their amazing sales, it is not by giving us simple chemical realities or by teaching us to observe fine distinctions but by giving us delightfully intense whiffs of the paradise of loving and being loved.

MUSCLE SENSATIONS

But in enhancing the image of the world and the self, the really big show is the sensations from our mucles. We maintain the tone of our inner self largely through the way in which we contract and relax specific muscles or the muscular system as a whole. How much we "feel like ourselves" depends on the familiarity or unfamiliarity of the message that our muscles are delivering to us at the moment. After a long illness, no matter what the signs of full medical recovery, the physician must deal with those habitual slumps and hypochondrias that go with habituation to bed and invalidism. The psychoanalyst can disarm our forcible forgetfulness by spreading us on a couch in which the ordinary "tightening up" of personal encounter is minimized. Not seeing the analyst, the patient surrenders some of his personal stance of readiness for a competitive encounter. Indeed he may go much further, and may battle less and less against his own memories.

Not even the "hysterical" blindness and deafness of hypnosis can build a wall as strong as that made by our tightened muscles against a reality we dread. We drum with our fingers, tap with our feet, squirm and writhe with arms and legs and trunk when unacceptable thoughts from the world of politics, religion, and personal memories, too vivid to be handled casually, "throw noise into the channel." Irregularity of breathing is a primary device for the generation of noise and is especially effective in blocking out unbearable arguments. The "inspiration-expiration" ratio (length of time spent "breathing in" divided by time spent in "breathing out") increases. We gasp in the uptake as we prepare a rebuttal. We swallow and heave, although not as well as is done on the stage, for all the dramatic effects of everyday life need to be blown up for theatrical display. The man or woman who can interfere with breathing activities in their socially expressive form can blot out awareness of even the most formidable reality. The systematic *control* of breathing, as in yoga, can go still further and can alter consciousness so that no ordinary message can be received. Much can be done very quietly by shifting the tongue about in the mouth, a quasi-cud-chewing operation, or by rubbing the skin of the forehead or cheek or chin. This may offer a distraction; or better yet, it may be done specifically to symbolize aggressive counterthreats to that which threatens us. The cudchewer and savage biter may develop enormous jaw muscles —"masseter muscle hypertrophy"—that is, he may act as if he wanted to "bite the world in two," as Paul Guggenheim suggests. Similarly, the act of turning away from an unbearable scene may actually appear in a chronic aversion of the eyes or the head.

THE ATTACK UPON MEMORY

It is important to stress that this inner "busy work" is directed against both immediate perception and memory. In general, memory is more compliant, more easily reduced to silence, than the direct perceptual world. It is partly a matter of individual skills. Some individuals known as hysterics may achieve magnificent blackouts, even over the perceptual world, while for most of us perceptual blackouts are possible only if the perceptions to be blotted out are extremely low in intensity, vague, and of short duration, so as to allow easier "autistic" control. Memory, however, unless we are struggling against hallucinatory vividness, is more easily subverted, if not the first time, then by repeated, insidious, and, later, massive attack. As Nietzsche puts it in *Beyond Good and Evil:* "My memory says I did it. My pride says I could not have done it, and in the end my memory yields."

In general, the attack upon memory is articulate, orderly, and well structured. Sooner or later, what is to be rooted out is fairly well rooted out. There are times, however, when the pain of a tragic memory is too intense and does not seem to yield at all, and times when, perhaps through a need for self-punishment, the disturbing memory is actually magnified during the process of struggle against it. One thinks of poor Oedipus, who, instead of effacing his painful memories, was impelled to blind himself, as if to make the ghastly memories still more overwhelming. Perhaps because the obliteration of the sunny, happy world of Greece had to be effectively carried through in order to give the painful memory a still greater punitive value, the Greek audience, and indeed all audiences confronted with the material of the Oedipus story, have felt forced not only to relive the horrible, the libidinal episodes for which punishment was due but also to relive the pain. The utter blackness of the blinded old man recapitulates or exaggerates the reality within us. One reason why the Oedipus situation, I think, is so tragic is its evocation of the impossibility of *un*remembering, the impossibility of obliterating memories that represent our failure to live sublimely and without guilt as man and woman should live.

No one has the strength to do this alone. In order to create the innocent blindness that carries us through the dark woods without fear of robbers, the deafness that makes us unable to hear a frightening cry, we must have about us those who deeply need the same protection, those who share with us our intense hope to march unfrightened into the dark. We need those who have been trained with us in a fraternity and a sorority of nonobservation, or indeed trained by us, and we by them, in a conspiracy of innocence.

But the ability to see reality also needs support. The point about the boy in the Hans Christian Andersen story "The Emperor's New Clothes" might have been quite different if there had been another little boy who challenged his vision of reality. The children who hear the story read aloud to them share with their parents the sense of this ridiculous old emperor, these wicked, cheating tailors. These silly grownups do not have the common sense that *we*, who see through it all, can display.

THE TONES OF STRANGE LANGUAGES

How deeply self-deception is ingrained is suggested by the impossibility of ever really hearing the range of vocal qualities produced by those whose mother tongue is different from our own. We can hear their words, but the tones of their language are alien to us. They have organized the world of communication by means of a massively different use of their speech equipment and, indeed, of their whole bodies. You can never make your tongue, soft palate, lips, or respiratory system work to sound like a Frenchman's or a German's or a Russian's. You cannot form the right sounds after the first few years of life, since you cannot really *hear* them; you do not make the differentiations at the right points. Notice also how speakers of other languages, when learning English, fail to differentiate the different kinds of a's and r's that are so characteristic of spoken English and that differ from the a's and r's of French and German and some other languages. The trouble with the flower girl who becomes "My Fair Lady" is that she cannot at first hear the sounds that her teacher wants her to hear. She belongs to the street world. That is the way she hears, and that is the way she articulates.

Father Curran of Loyola University in Chicago is among those who have solved the problem of noncommunication that faces those who want to learn to speak foreign languages. Curran's method, simplified here, is to seat at a table a Frenchman, a German, and an Italian, ready to learn English, together with an American. The American may be considered the teacher. His tablemates, however, are engaged in meaningful conversation; they are not just "learning to speak English." They ask real questions and get real answers about matters of general interest. The heat is taken off. They are not "right" or "wrong" in anything they say, any more than a person in an ordinary friendly conversation would be "right" or "wrong." Their situation is like that of a little child who is concerned with what he wants to say, and not with whether it is "right" or not. And, incidentally, how little attention he pays when he is "corrected"; the important thing is to convey meanings and get results. It is meaning, not phonetics, that counts. Indeed, one has to guess, with Curran's method, who is the teacher; nor is the prompt learning of "correct" English necessary. Much more progress results from this functional use of language than from the attempt to eradicate errors. As with the small child, the adult's real aim is to convey meaning. There is social approval, but it is low-key approval. It comes automatically when the primary accent is on communication. Before long, an interesting discussion of the real differences between sounds can be initiated.

A very important part of the method is the matter of *equality* with the others at the table. We are not dealing with the preceptor-pupil situation, a situation in which one's own efforts are praised or condemned. Our concern is with a way to become aware of the blindness and deafness of solitary self-deception, sharing with one's fellows the social need for a communication that has been blocked, learning through a group endeavor.

Indeed, it may be that individual psychotherapy is sometimes wide of the mark by clinging to the disciplinary role of the preceptor, who in the nature of the case has to be "right." The meetings of any and all groups who have the solution for the worlds' ills, whether at the level of psychotherapy, education, science, or world affairs, seem to suggest that the task lies not in the remodeling of the individual mind or heart but in the redefinition of the social membership roles, which all members of the group must simultaneously and in mutual dependence accept and work through.

EXAMPLES FROM ANTHROPOLOGY

The anthropologist, observing peoples whose folkways differ profoundly from his own, attempts "scientific objectivity." He may in some measure achieve it. He strives not to disvalue a preliterate group. He may, however, like Bateson and Mead in *Balinese Character*, understand the group life as he shares his thoughts with another observer. The photographic documentation supplied in this case makes it possible to glimpse the collective awareness and the collective blindness that come from the very nature of the situation. The text brings out relationships regarding which the photographs are mute, but the photographs sometimes eloquently say much that is lost in the verbal narrative. The case is saved to some degree for science by the fact that the biases, even of a husband and wife trained in the same professional observational skills, cannot perfectly match one another. It is through seeing the match between the two in light of the mismatch that one knows an approximation to reality was achieved.

Another example from anthropology: not long after World War II, I had the privilege of talking with an anthropologist responsible for the social-science education of a group of American officers, who, in turn, had responsibility for administrative control over a large number of island groups in the Pacific. He had the task of familiarizing American officers with anthropology; he hoped that they would look with more objective eyes on the "primitive people." Actually, no such happy consummation was easily attainable. The American administrators *did* indeed quickly learn to take a scientific point of view regarding the people of the Pacific. What they could *not* learn was to take a similar point of view regarding the people of the United States, including themselves! They had learned to look upon the civilization of the United States as a sort of standard. Indeed, since they shared this world with other Americans, they probably encountered their own half-perceived difficulty in communicating with other American administrators as a matter of petty inconvenience but not as a danger sign regarding the likelihood of profound disorientation and bias. The American administrators could not possibly have learned to look upon American culture in those simple and detached frames of reference, in which they expected to understand the "primitive" people of the Pacific islands.

Blindness has many dimensions. It is organized in depth; it is heavily redundant. Social life is so contrived as to prevent successful penetration of the thick capsule that normally surrounds the observer. E. G. Boring, in a celebrated study

[43]

"The Psychology of Controversy," noted how, time and again, brilliant opponents, each armed with his group of disciples, managed to miss the reality of a psychological situation. Each man, supported by his lieutenants, was immune to re-education. It was the quiet little newcomer like our boy in the Hans Christian Andersen story who crept softly into the middle of the fray and pointed out the reality that no one else had been able to see.

Sometimes it is the individual, but sometimes it is the group, who excels in the blindness of self-deception. When Freud was confronted with the fact that the great Charcot could not see the sexuality in hysterical behavior, he said, "Yes, but if he knows this, why does he never say so?" The two or three other authorities whom Freud consulted had the same blindness. It took the lonely Freud, addressing a local medical society, to see and to say what the collective wisdom and the collective seeing power of medicine could not see.

It might be worthwhile to raise at this point the question of possible cross-cultural teaching. Americans could be taught by groups of preliterates who would serve as "informants" on American life; psychologists might be taught by their pupils, especially their foreign pupils, regarding some of the intimacies of preparation for the systematic nonseeing which is a vital part of all professional training.

In summary, all humanity faces much that is repugnant. We must see as our group sees, and beyond that there are differences springing from individual needs. We need blinders to prevent "distraction," so that we can function in our daily lives without fear and the evidence of defeat. And because terror and defeat are partly defined in individual terms, we need custom-built blinders to prevent interference with the special viewpoint we have undertaken to maintain.

So it begins to look as if we had been trying to write *Hamlet* without the Prince of Denmark. The devices for selecting and filtering, structuring and unifying the system of defenses hardly ever operate in the rather mechanical fashion that was suggested up to the point at which the *self* entered the discussion. The exclusion of information is in very large part guaranteed by another central device—the building up of a picture of the self, to be forever enhanced and defended.

CHAPTER 5

―――――

Self-Deception and
the Laboratory

For Socrates, a central problem of philosophy was to "Know Thyself." He was speaking of the self as conveyed by perception, memory, and reason, by conversation with colleagues, and by some deep sense of cultural destiny of which one is a part. We of the twentieth century have other possibilities of knowing ourselves, possibilities that are constantly broadening. Our next step in trying to spell out the problem of self-deception is to show that by modern feedback studies we can discover *how* we are deceiving ourselves and can use much of the technical expertise of modern science in the process of looking inside us, as Socrates would have done if the tools had been available in his time.

On certain days we suspect that there may be something wrong inside: butterflies in the stomach or a lump or a bump or a ringing in the ears, or an unexplained chronic distress, which we say to ourselves might be "partly psychological" but has "some organic basis." We make an appointment with the doctor. He may be able to infer a good deal from what he sees and from what you tell him. His face, we think, begins to show a tentative decision. He says all that he feels he can say, then adds, "We'll wait for the lab tests." You and he assume that by analyzing your blood and urine, as well as by listening to your heart, taking your blood pressure, and by performing various mysteries which you do not fully understand, he will piece together an interpretation. You hope that the integration of all this information will give a clear picture and suggest a clear and successful program to lead you back to health. He is getting "inside information." Indeed, if he uses a fluoroscope he actually does "look inside you." He may even want to freeze the momentary impressions into more enduring form, and take X rays, which he will discuss with experts in X-ray work. The X rays will be part of the objective record of your insides at that particular time.

He has other delicate instruments that complete his kind of inside picture. There is the oscilloscope, with its jagged brilliant lines like forked lightning, which you have learned, from television, to know and respect, for it gives you electronic information about the activities of muscle and brain. He may show you visible evidence that your tightened muscles are producing new types of jagged lines on the oscilloscope and that muscular relaxation may quickly iron out many of your kinks and achieve an almost miraculous straightening where "every mountain and hill shall be made low . . . and the rough places plain." He may point out how your brain waves, shown in the electroencephalograph, may change moment by moment as you relax, and he may have occasion to study the changed form of these brain waves as you indulge in a fantasy or daydream. Or you may even be among those whom he invites to his "sleep and dream laboratory" for a night's study of your brain-wave patterns in conjunction with the rapid eye movements that occur during your dreaming episodes. From a classical study of pulse and temperature to these more complex modern electronic lines of evidence, he is relentlessly pursuing and tracking into odd corners all the available evidence about what is going on in your inner world. Combining all this with your

[47]

verbal reports of what you remember or imagine or feel, he knows the total biological *you* in far richer detail and in far greater scope than the medical man of the mid–nineteenth century could have done.

SOURCES OF INNER INFORMATION

One of the most interesting things about this pursuit of inside information is the discovery of the ways in which you yourself are blocking from your own observation the rich information that is constantly coming in. Among the most important of all sources of information about ourselves are the tensions in our muscles, partly because these tensions tell us what we are about to do, and partly because we play some muscles against others—we tighten up at some point in order to keep ourselves from knowing what activities we are getting ready to perform or would like to perform or are afraid we might perform. For we keep from ourselves the living record of our tendencies to action; so it is not just benign ignorance but a game we continuously play to keep ourselves from knowing what our muscles are up to. We know that we are tense, and that is about all we know. Look at the oscilloscope, however, and you can see which muscles are tense, when they become tense, and when they relax. And you can, through a kind of training (to be described later), learn to open the channels of information about the self. You may learn to look within and see how, by tightening our muscles in a way called "rigidity," we may shut out flexible, moving, and vital sources of information that might disturb our everyday equanimity.

All over the country, of course, closed-circuit television is being used to give a person visual feedback of his acts at the very time they occur, so that he sees himself even better than he could in a mirror. Thus, retarded adolescents are being helped to see, through television, where they are making awkward, mistaken social approaches to people. Particularly dramatic, I think, is what M. L. Johnson Abercrombie, a British zoologist, did in 1966 while teaching medical students how to read X rays. She brought out not only the things that the students missed but the things that they missed inside themselves that caused them to misread the X rays. In other words, she brought together in a feedback study inside information, outside information, and the crossroads where they meet in the process of developing one's biased interpretation. One fears to see a malignant indicator, one is prone to see a particular kind of evidence, one is defensive lest one make a mistake. One is able to mobilize both the exteroceptive functions—the use of eye, ear, skin—which give misfocused and misleading information, and the interoceptive information that pours in all the time from within the body, which we ordinarily misread, denying the rapid pulse, the fury, the passion, and the fears for one reason or another. We are poor at scanning the internal information; we fail to see how the internal confusion and the external confusion reinforce one another. But it is possible to study human moods by training both the observer and the subject himself to see how he is misreading both what is outside and what is inside—both the evidence of so-called objective science and the evidence of internal input, called "proprioceptive." This internal input includes a variety of forms of information regarding the subject's so-called phenomenal or subjective world.

EVOLUTIONARY PSYCHOLOGY

We seem to have overlooked this extraordinary human capacity for shutting out information because we have not seen in perspective the contribution of Charles Darwin and of evolutionary thinking generally. Darwin's volumes *The Origins of Species, The Descent of Man,* and *The Expression of the Emotions in Man and Animals* might tempt us to think that a true Darwinian evolutionary psychology would be very simple. Natural selection should logically give us the best possible eyes for seeing, the best possible ears for hearing, and the best possible brains and muscles serving these sense organs, so as to put us directly and neatly in touch with all that is out there in our environment. Those organisms that have good eyes and ears, good connecting systems, brains, muscles, and so forth, would be most realistically in touch with their environment. If we say only this, however, we neglect what many of the early evolutionists clearly saw. The British neurologist F. Hughlings-Jackson pointed out that the more recently developed organs of the bodily system are often unstable, inefficient, and subject to breakdown, and of course the brain, particularly the higher and evolutionarily *recent* parts of the brain, is especially subject to such difficulties. Today, in terms of information theory, we talk about "overload," which prevents adequate and realistic use of our brains in seeing, remembering, and thinking, as is surely evident in both experimental and clinical studies of human perception. Along with overload there is frequently, as the information theorist would say, "noise" interfering with the effective use of the "channel," as discussed earlier.

There are, in evolutionary terms, many reasons why we should expect the perceptual system to be far from perfect; in fact, it is frequently so organized as to fight against perfection, to prevent the receipt of full-fledged, clear, errorless information. Of course, we do not really need to go so far in our demonstration of the failures of perception, because it is well known from animal experimentation and from naturalistic studies of animals in their ordinary environment that they are misled by illusions; they misjudge sizes and distances, for example, just as we do. In fact, one major branch of evolutionary psychology is the study of the proneness of animals to be deceived by the "camouflage" of their prey or predators. Their eyes and ears, though biologically refined and effective, are misled through the natural selection which has made their prey so marvelously effective against the predators' perceptual resources. There are, we should add, though, not only these very primitive responses to camouflage and countercamouflage in nature but also many cases in which the emotional life of the animal—as, for example, through its fury or its fear—sensitizes it to misleading cues. At the human level this proneness to emotional distortion of cues from the environment is further complicated by cultural factors, which make us stand together, so to speak, against unwanted information.

GENERIC VERSUS INDIVIDUALIZED PERCEPTION

So we have come full circle. We have encountered in the evolutionist's own land reasons why built-in "errors" in sensory perception have occurred and been fortified. In a recent volume by George S. Klein, *Perception, Motives, and Personality*, we are confronted at the beginning with these two approaches to perception: one emphasizing what might be called the generic way of perceiving and one emphasizing what might be called the individualized way of perceiving. Klein shows why a mature psychology must thoroughly integrate both ways of viewing human perceptual responses. Since well over 99 percent of the research on perception is concerned with reality functions, it is a bit strange that even calling attention to the reality-missing forms of perception is often regarded as an "exaggeration." It is very doubtful whether one can make a generalization about the relative importance of reality-missing kinds of perceiving. After all, we must keep in mind the wide range of human cultures and of human individuality, as well as the role of self-correcting habits, comparing senses with each other in the direction of "consensual validation" and the long years that are spent in correcting perceptions of various sorts. It is doubtful whether a generalization, a "box score" regarding the errors of perceiving, would serve any purpose. It is important, however, when gross errors in self-understanding occur, that we make maximum use of the reality orientation that we need in order to see clearly what we are doing with, and to, ourselves when we are blind to our own blindness.

The cultural aspect of the problem calls for special emphasis. One sees partly in terms of the requirements of information coming from outside but partly in terms of avoiding the stress, the inner response to our feeling of wrongness with regard to the cultural code. We see ourselves as out of line because we have not seen as others see. All the mechanisms of psychoanalytic and other dynamic psychiatries become relevant in showing the devices by which not only memory and thought but perception itself is enriched with evasive self-deceptive devices. What Freud described as "secondary process" as a phase of the process of "reality-testing" clarifies why reality is often so hard to come by. Indeed, even in the midst of a serious concern with finding reality, much of the blocking process is at work, which makes it doubtful whether a pure regard for reality is ever found. There are indeed, as Heinz Hartmann lucidly showed, "conflict-free" areas, which are concerned with true adaptation to the environment, and in these areas the curiosity drive (to which we shall return) can play a major part. And curiosity, once set afire, can blaze furiously indeed but may lead to overemphasis here, underemphasis there, while at the same time, lively curiosity about what is outside may coexist with the blocking process going on within.

The escape from the distress of seeing ourselves as we really are may in fact be a chronic need, since most of us live in societies in which we may well be wrong but cannot afford to know we are wrong. We certainly cannot afford to attend closely to the devices by which socially defined wrongness and rightness contend within us.

SOME EXPERIMENTAL EVIDENCE

If asked for the evidence to support our view of self-deception—that it consists of perceptual distortion along with memory and thought distortion—we could list three main classes of evidence:

First, we should mention the altered relations of "figure and ground." Whatever you see at the moment, engaging your attention, stands out with a certain amount of structure, called figure; the ground, or background, is relatively unorganized. In musical compositions, there typically is a *leitmotiv*, and then there are subordinate and enriching tonal materials, which supply the context. Figure and ground often shift. If you take, for example, those devices which the cartoonist likes to use in newspapers, when one tries to find the "four Indians and the three cowboys" in a tangle of lines, typically one thing after another will take its turn as figure.

The terms "figure and ground" come to us from the Danish psychologist E. Rubin, who showed that there are definite dynamic laws that determine in a black-and-white pattern what forms will stand out as figure with definite structure and meaning, and what will remain as background at a lower level of organization. The church on the hill, for example, is ordinarily figure, and the hillside is ground. This is not just a question of what you attend to, either, for you can attend to a tree or a lawn or the blue sky near the church, and the church may still retain its primary value as figure. This will depend partly on prior exposure, of course, and partly upon your attitude or set at the time. We are not considering the entire systematic psychology of figure and ground here, but just one particular phenomenon that is highly important for our present theory—namely, the fact that figure-and-ground relations are to a considerable degree alterable through prior experience involving *gratifications* and *frustrations*. The role of reward and punishment stands out quite explicitly in the experiments of Roy Schafer at City College. Schafer used vertical contour lines and dots for the eyes to represent stylized cartoon-type human faces, as in Figure 3. At one-third of a second exposure, the figure to the left was shown to certain subjects with the instruction that they learn that

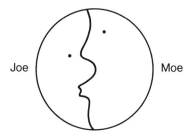

Figure 3. Figure and Ground.

the name of this individual was "Joe"; to other individuals the other half of the circle was shown with the instruction that they learn that the name was "Moe." To the first group, without any explanation, a few coins were given as Joe was shown, and a few coins taken away when Moe was shown; and the procedure was reversed with other subjects, who were thus "rewarded" for Moe, "punished" for Joe. After sixteen such presentations, strong figure-ground organization had been built up, so that now, when the *full circle* was quickly shown, each subject predominantly saw the face for which he had been rewarded, rather than the face for which he had been punished. Indeed, some subjects made caustic comments upon the punished face; it was a poorly drawn face, an "idiot," and so forth (though accepted without comment by those rewarded).

Auditory figure-ground studies have likewise been done. Two experimenters took turns in reading aloud to our subjects at The Menninger Foundation paragraphs from Rachel Carson's *The Sea Around Us*. While one voice was reading, a few nickels were pushed at the subject. While the other voice was reading, the subject lost nickels. "Counterbalanced" subjects were rewarded where the others were punished, and vice versa. To a significant degree, when subjects listened to a tape containing a mixture of the two voices, they heard one voice; that was the voice that had been associated with winning the money.

As far as we know, the Schafer-Murphy principle holds for a variety of visual, tactual and auditory situations, although Eleanor Gibson in her *Principles of Perceptual Learning and Development* disagrees with us.

DIRECTIONAL EFFECTS

A second kind of device available in self-deception studies is to allow oneself to be pulled in one direction while dragging one's feet when drawn in other directions. We might say simply that the person takes, in physical space, or in the world of his surroundings or among his memories, a direction that is congenial and gratifying. A convenient way to explore this sort of thing is the "autokinetic effect," the apparent movement of a stationary point of light in a pitch-black room (cf. pp. 7–8). Although actual physical movement does not occur, under the usual laboratory conditions, the light "moves" for most people, especially when a verbal suggestion is used.

Harold Voth and his collaborators at the Menninger Foundation have shown that the light tends to move a great deal for those who are fantasy-rich or imaginative in a broad sense, or withdrawn or locked up in themselves. People with normal fantasies can allow themselves a very considerable amount of movement. Some people, however, simply do not see the light move at all. They seem to be "ultrarealistic" in the sense that they are out there in physical reality, and since the light is not really moving at all, they, as the "reality seekers," see no movement. It might seem to follow that these are the *real* reality people. But in point of fact, many of them are inclined to run away from their inner selves, and their problems, by becoming intensely preoccupied with the outer world. They may be inclined more to a determined kind of reality seeking than to the healthy, normal, fantasy-rich play of the imagination in which there is room for balance between outer and inner concerns. For the present, our main interest is in the fact that there are these *different* *ways* of seeking reality.

Can one expect some people to pursue the light when that means something good for them and avoid it when the light has negative implications? This is what Bobby Farrow achieved in an ingenious experiment in which the subject learned to see the light and its movement in terms of the hypothesis that it will go wherever there is gratification for the observer. So firmly were the associations formed that when, later, the *stationary* light was shown, it moved for the subject into those areas that were free of associated shock, and it would not move into those areas in which shock was associated with the position of the light. The light "kept out of trouble." This is what we mean by a "directional factor," or letting oneself move in a rewarded direction. Similar studies indicate that rewarded material becomes *vivid*, while nonrewarded or punished material becomes dim or obscure.

LOOK–AVOIDANCE

A third kind of perceptual avoidance is illustrated in studies of "looking." Lester Luborsky and his collaborators in Philadelphia have done intriguing experiments, with beautiful modern techniques for studying eye movements, on the ways in which one avoids *looking* in troubled areas. Individual differences in this area were found to be especially great. If you take the psychoanalytic system defining idiosyncrasies in terms of defense mechanisms, you note, for example, that the "isolators"—the people who can pocket off each little stimulus pattern from its context—can bear to look at a certain picture *provided* that the context and emotional tone are shut out. In the experiment the clinical isolators actually do isolate in the perceptual test. They turn out to have different "looking habits" from the "repressors." The relative failure to use the whole of the total context presented ties in nicely with psychoanalytic conceptions of defense—with actual self-deceptive problems in looking.

So fundamental is the looking process that a couple of our Australian friends, visiting me and my colleagues in Topeka, decided that they could get what they wanted regarding personality measurements by studying the way in which the subject responded to aversive pictures. These were colored reproductions of tragic or disturbing paintings attached to the four corners of a very large display, with an X–Y plotter that greatly magnified the vertical and horizontal sweep of the eyes. Thus the subjects could freely scan while actually avoiding what they did not want to see.

One item, for example, in this large mass of pictures, which turned up while I was acting as a preliminary subject, was a picture of the martyrdom of Saint Sebastian. If you have this Renaissance painting of Saint Sebastian, you know that he is riddled with arrows. This was shown in great detail. You would think that if one looked very carefully and at close range at this large picture, the flow of the blood and the evidence of suffering would be striking. I always found it quite a good deal to take. What I saw on this occasion was a foot—perhaps a clubfoot—and a beautiful velvety-red background, which had been created for some artistic purpose that I did not understand.

[57]

What is important about my own self-deception is that I managed to see almost nothing of the stressful situation. My eye movements in other directions were quite free, with a good sweep, as long as I did not look at the troubling areas. Later on, when I was asked to recall the picture, my eyes employed another curious device, which was to jig around; that is to say, to do a lot of "busy work" without really looking.

We then began looking for a name for these phenomena and kept thinking of the many different ways that exist of *not seeing*. The eyes can see, but they are also expert in nonseeing. We remembered the title that e. e. cummings gave to his public addresses when he was asked to lecture at Harvard. He replied that he did not "lecture." So the talks were published under the title *Six Non-Lectures*. Following the analogy, we decided that the eye was the organ of nonseeing, and that afternoon we defined many different ways in which the eyes can be used for nonseeing (without including variations in pupillary size). These, in colloquial English, include looking away, jigging around, blurring, glaring, looking straight through you, shutting out ("scotoma" or "hysterical gating-out"), and figure-ground reversal.

We can summarize the chapter so far by saying that self-deception begins with a perceptual phenomenon of limiting input. Then, because of threats to the person's drive realization or some fears about his self-image, the limitation of input is affected rather largely by scotoma, control of emphasis, and figure-ground mechanisms.

ATTENTION

How is attention related to the exclusion of information to protect the self? Here we may direct our investigation to the concept of scanning. You may think of the sailor in the crow's nest with his binoculars looking for icebergs or submarines or any form of danger as developing a certain expertise in the capacity to scan—a skill that marks the difference between a new sailor and an old salt. We see something like this in the good and the poor proofreader. There must be individual differences in attending that would relate to competence in scanning. It should all be local, let us say, in the eye muscles as such. We should think, as Piaget does, about the process of *centration*, a sort of machine-gun volley of acts of attending toward some things and attending away from others. Retrospectively, centration should fit into the figure-ground type of study, the autokinetic type of study, and the study of scotomatizing pictures. We might then be able to pin a good part of the responsibility for self-deception on the scanning processes: "What kinds of information are you looking for?"

It is important to emphasize that we do not necessarily *distort*. It may sometimes be necessary to distort, as I have tried to suggest, but it may be just as simple to exclude. When Lois Murphy and I were in India, working for UNESCO and studying the Hindu-Muslim conflict, we found that a good deal of the tension that could be located in regard to the so-called riots—often terrible affairs—that would break out between these two communities was not a matter of distorted information. Rather, it was simply a matter of not encountering an important part of the information. We found that the news read by the Muslims gave an adequate perspective and good "justification" for enormous hostility to the Hindu community, and vice versa. The same probably held true of much of the information offered about the Vietnamese conflict, since the system involved in the selection of news gave adequate supports for conduct from a clear and coherent viewpoint.

We thought we might be able to shed some light on the delicate process of scanning, and to see in particular how habits of scanning are learned. We used Topeka elementary-school children in our experiment. We placed recessed panels at the corners of a yard-square board, wherein little white animal figures appeared. For each child, four of the figures were randomly assigned to the different positions, and all the child had to do was to name the animal. But, of course, any animal might appear at any of the four points. We used a reinforcement schedule in which 70 percent of the time when the child named a particular animal, we said "right," "okay," "that's it," "couldn't fool you," or some such mildly supportive remark. The other three animals were reinforced at a 30-percent frequency.

We quickly observed a tendency for the child to move toward selecting, using, and naming the animal that led to the warm support from the adult. We thought this could be called operant conditioning of the process of attending. To be sure this was not just a conditioning of eye movements as such, we made a search panel, in which all forty of the animals were used in a strip, and the child was asked to find rapidly each of the animals as the names were called out. The child found the things that he had been socially rewarded for seeing much more rapidly than the others. This is "learning transfer," of a sort, involving a change in spatial relationships. Apparently the tasks involved something more than just eye movements, for the child had been trained to develop and hold a specific set and could find more quickly that which had been integrated with his own system of satisfactions.

CHAPTER 6

The Role of the
Voluntary Muscles

AT ABOUT the time that some of us at the Menninger Foundation were working on the problems of scanning, others were concerned with another activity that normal people carry out to avoid confronting reality head on, namely, bracing against stressful information, becoming rigid, both psychologically and muscularly. We had noticed that during "defense" there were tightened muscles, of the sort that Reich had described as an accompanying symptom to certain types of "character armor," and we suspected that people were "scotomatizing" partly by muscular contractions, which interfered with perceptual responses by throwing "noise" into the channel. This discovery led us to the idea that the child or adult may *learn* how to tighten up at a critical moment, *in order to throw noise into the channel* and to keep out damaging information. We turned our attention to the voluntary muscles of the arms, neck, and back, beginning particularly with the forearms, for which we could get good electromyographic evidence as to what was going on. We could find out what degree of relaxation of these muscles would let in the excluded information.

RELAXATION AND MEMORY

There are many kinds of psychotherapy for relaxing muscles that have been tightened against information, including E. Jacobson's "progressive relaxation" and the methods used by J. Schultz in Germany and by W. Luthe in Montreal. There seems to be abundant evidence that the cultivation of skill in relaxation can have a good deal to offer in this problem.* It struck us that maybe one could teach a person to bring in perceptual information, memory information, and information relating to the thought processes by relaxing him in a disciplined way, *if* he could learn—and this was the whole core of the problem for us—to utilize the information from his muscles. Could he watch himself getting tense? Could he, by a suitable relaxation technique, discover that he has been excluding information that he could accept? In other words, could he begin to see the process of self-deception in terms of the removal of those barriers, those tightenings, those rigidities, that have been playing their part all along in the exclusion of highly relevant information?

A Norwegian psychiatrist, Trygve Braatoy, must be credited with very brilliant work on this problem. His is one of the earliest applications of the Reichian concept of "character armor" to the problem of opening the channels of information as to what one's muscles are doing. Braatoy found a number of men with "arm neuroses," in which the arms were tight and painful. The men presented a clinical picture that suggested, first, extensor involvement, as if the men wanted to fight, but, second, flexor involvement, something holding them back. When, with a combination of verbal therapy and a good deal of physical therapy, the muscles were rather suddenly relaxed, there were in some cases "floods

* We are bypassing the fact that muscles, tendons, and joints work together. To avoid getting into technical detail, we use the term "muscle" to refer to the system of muscles, tendons, and joints.

of painful memories." It does not take very deep analytic study to come to the conclusion that these memories included fantasies and impulses toward violent retaliation against the father, fantasies earlier incapable of gaining access to consciousness and locked into this particular anatomical and physiological pattern of rigidity.

A good deal of our thinking, then, was related to this type of phenomenon and to other studies of clinical rigidity that suggested to us that through relaxation technique not just floods of painful memories but also information about oneself might come in. Indeed there might come information about the devices by which one was preventing such information from coming in. If this happened to be correct, there would be several other parts of the body that would join in. The respiratory system is particularly important here, and Bjørn Christiansen, a pupil and colleague of Braatoy, has given much time to the respiratory patterns that differentiate persons who show different types of conflict and different types of exclusion techniques—the sudden catching of the breath, the gasp, very shallow or very rapid breathing. We recognize them all from the stage. Earlier, we saw that manipulation of the respiratory rate, often completely unconsciously, is a marvelous device for throwing noise into the system and also that it has certain specific purposes, as the gasp of Othello. It may be local, specific, and purposive, as well as diffuse and explosive. Consequently, drawing attention *per se* might not eliminate the exclusion technique, but retraining the person to control breathing rate might do so.

Up to this point, then, exclusion techniques might involve the voluntary musculature of the arms, hands, trunk, neck, forehead, and, by implication, other large skeletal muscles of the body, notably those in the respiratory and speech systems and those involved in the positioning of the head and the eyes, as well as the obvious flexor and extensor movements of hands, arms, and facial muscles. The actor, the portrait painter, the anthropologist have told us a great deal about the processes by which muscles are tightened to the point of actual stiffness during periods of rejecting information.

We suspected also that the "involuntary" musculature of the cardiovascular system, the gastrointestinal system, and some other action systems was also involved, and we remembered a long series of studies in which relaxation of involuntary muscles has been used in connection with opening up the subject's field of operations to give him a greater awareness and greater control of his activities. So we suspected that the seeking and scanning studies of Luborsky and associates and of our own Menninger Foundation group, as well as many others, were all cutting across this field in various ways.

BREATHING PATTERNS

Christiansen made studies of twelve women patients compared with twelve C. F. Menninger Hospital nurses who cared for them, each individual coming to our laboratory for a leisurely investigation of breathing patterns and of the circulatory patterns associated with them. He found quite large differences between the patients and the comparison group. The nurses gave familiar respiratory curves. The twelve patients gave a grossly different breathing pattern. From the huge literature organized by Christiansen, compared with these fresh data, it seemed reasonable to conclude that irregularities in breathing were largely defensive, associated with interrupting oneself as one thinks or talks, breathing too deeply, holding one's breath too long, or a dozen other patterns less cleanly rhythmical than one ordinarily obtains. (One may think here of "sub-breathing stammerers," who at a critical point fail to breathe deeply enough to get the oxygen they need.) Of course the connection of breathing with the process of blockage or repression is much more complex than we are now able to spell out; hyperventilation, for example, and hypoventilation may cause abnormal levels of oxygen utilization in the brain and may induce a trance or various mystical states long known to Indian and Japanese practitioners.

UNCONSCIOUS TRAINING

These various types of relaxation with feedback, leading to the conception of systematic control of the "voluntary" muscle system, enabled Ralph Hefferline at Columbia University to conceive the ingenious idea that people might be trained (without their *knowledge*) to produce a change in the environment in accordance with their needs or wishes. His equipment was arranged so that a slight movement of the thumb would provide a signal that led to the elimination of the unpleasant hum in a radio passage of music. The subjects thus trained did not know that it was their own activity that led to the elimination of this unpleasant hum. S. David Kahn, a psychiatrist in Atlanta, has used a tiny muscle group in the hand (at the base of the little finger) which by an electronic arrangement will switch back and forth the visual presentation, a figure-and-ground display, in front of the subject's eyes. Unwittingly the subject begins more and more to activate these little muscles so as to see the picture that he wants, and to block out the alternative picture. The figure-ground reversal is achieved simply by controlling these small muscles in the palm of the hand. This, then, is a literal case of unconscious exclusion of input and encouragement of other input at the same time. It is analogous to the "looking" studies and the earliest figure-ground studies of Schafer and of Jackson, which are discussed in Chapter 5, but it is both conceptually and instrumentally different in the matter of the subject's own control of the functioning channels of information from the external world.

Most of the work described is quite recent and calls for replication. Actually, however, many of the working principles come from ancient systems of observation and thought; notably, those of India and Japan. Much closely related work has also been done in the physiological laboratories of the Soviet Union, in a somewhat different scientific atmosphere from that which prevails in most of our own laboratories. There is a mixture of warm welcome and fairly firm skepticism when psychophysiological research of this sort in one cultural area is scanned by investigators in a very different setting. But part of this is sheer provincialism and unawareness of work going on across linguistic and cultural barriers.*

Regarding this matter of the credibility of psychophysiological reports from different cultural areas, it is useful to remember the journey made by M. A. Wenger and B. K. Bagchi to study adepts in yoga in various ashrams in India. Among well-trained yogi, there were cases of verbal self-reports of complete stoppage of the heart. The instruments' records, however, showed the heart still at work. There is probably no question about sincerity; rather, the question is a matter of the degree of sensitivity, or threshold level. The heartbeat was not vigorous enough to send evidence of itself to reach the conscious level. Nevertheless, the yogic relaxation produced some effect, and the more recent work involving collaboration of Indian and Western investigators, as in the work of B. K. Anand, suggests that with more sensitive equipment, a fully conscious response to very low activity levels may be achieved and adequately recorded. We have, after all, a striking modern development in J. V. Basmajian's success in bringing muscle tension down to the zero level. And we know that this is not in itself particularly mysterious, being a matter of

* Our own provincialism is exemplified in our referring mostly to English-language studies, but the reader has a right to as broad a view as he can develop. See, for example, *A Handbook of Contemporary Soviet Psychology*, Michael Cole and Irving Maltzman, eds. (New York: Basic Books, 1969).

feedback in the conscious subject who watches a panel, with its direct evidence of waxing and waning tension level.

Suppose, for example, you had in mind Erikson's "basic trust," or Rogers' idea of acceptance of the total person, or Robert White's idea of letting the mind do its own work, instead of cramping its style. You might be able, through the dissipation of such tensions, on a voluntary basis, to assist your subject to learn to reject the rejection process. That is to say, to learn to open up to a variety of sorts of information highly relevant to the way in which one perceives oneself. Of course, you would need time and skill to encounter and cope with each layer of muscular rigidity. The essential mechanism in this learning process is feedback; specifically, by these cases described, the subject will watch the panel and see how far he is succeeding.

The device by which this is accomplished is very simple: a meter shows the subject the degree of relaxation he has achieved. If you give him information regarding his relaxation, even in the course of fifteen or twenty minutes—according to present findings—the subject may eventually give you a *complete* relaxation of a given muscle in the sense that the curve is absolutely horizontal. The subject has mastered the task.

But we need to consider more closely what goes on in the feedback process.

THE ENDLESS FENCING GAME

In Chapters 3 to 5 we looked at the problem of the self-image and the process of protecting and enhancing that self-image against all threats. As children, each of us learned about the systems and organs of our bodies, and the sounds of our own voices, and soon thereafter the names assigned us and the expectations and responsibilities that go with our own individuality. We learned to see our behavior as a "reflection" on our name and the family name, and we accepted roles defined by the community. All that each of us aims to achieve becomes organized around this image of the self.

As Shakespeare has it in *Othello:*

> *Who steals my purse steals trash* . . .
> *But he that filches from me my good name*
> *Robs me of that which not enriches him,*
> *And makes me poor indeed.*

This is the tussle of reputation against reputation, the elementary "narcissistic" stance in a prestige-oriented society.

We ask each boy, each girl, to "face reality." How can they if they are facing, as fencing novices, the thrust and parry involved in maintaining a name? A primary problem for anyone who is concerned with facing reality is how to transcend the individual self-deceptions that go with this endless fencing game; to try to see individual styles and, here and there, general styles for encountering and escaping threats to the self-image. This means a central focus upon the one great counterweight which we may oppose to our dangers: the enormously deep and strong thrust toward reality that exists in normal people, which can be strengthened and refined.

THE REJECTION OF REJECTION

Perhaps as we get feedback from voluntary muscles, we become aware, however dimly, of the activities we are carrying out. But if now we are blocking our inner message system —that is, "throwing noise into the channel"—we are, to some degree, unaware of the local tensions involved; to some degree, unaware of the tightening of specific muscle groups. Insofar, then, as we are throwing noise into the channel, we are rejecting information. It follows that if there is a definite motive at work to try to understand an illusion or a logical error or to improve one's effectiveness in reality testing in any other way, one can *become alert* to perceive this kind of local noise. Suppose one learns that drumming with the fingers, tapping with the foot, and various similar mannerisms are used as devices for rejecting information. Once this has been learned, a countermovement is set up: to keep on the alert for noise in the system and to develop the basis for relaxation of those muscles, so as to clear the channel of such noise. One develops, in other words, the habit of clearing away the process of rejection. Just as the Islamic philosophers developed their theory of "the destruction of destruction," so we may say that our modern principle of "the rejection of rejection" becomes equivalent to Pavlov's familiar principle of the "inhibition of an inhibition."

Our aim, then, is to catch the signal that tells us we are rejecting reality and to respond in such a way as either to ignore it or to listen to it for the sake of new exploratory efforts at adaptation. Ordinarily, we do the former; that is, unless the desire for reality is quite strong, the first response to the unwelcome signal is to reject it. But if curiosity or any drive to reality is strong enough to dominate the situation, we proceed by trial and error in order to discover ways of eliminating the noise more and more efficiently. We would expect a normal motor learning process to appear by which an individual learns to confront, and ultimately to remove, noise from his own information channels.

An experimental program for the reduction of self-deception would have much in common with the approach of Frederick Perls, Ralph Hefferline, and Paul Goodman in their book *Gestalt Therapy*. Exploring the body as a whole, it would identify the locus, intensity, and temporal course of each significant noise, would note the shift in attention from one muscle group to another, and would attempt to get a systematic view of the defensive system, or "character armor," of each individual studied. In many cases, it would be discovered that local tension, let us say in the right forearm, is spreading to the left forearm, or even that it is spreading all over the body. It is likely, at least, that certain other systems, such as the neck, the speech organs, and the eyes would regularly be involved in an operation of any degree of complexity. Much of the program of Perls, Hefferline, and Goodman could pass from the clinical to the experimental level.

MUSCLES AS GENERATORS OF NOISE

Our conclusion so far is that the voluntary (striped) muscles are constantly playing a part in shutting out information. Our primary interest continues to lie in the noise function, which is destroying or inhibiting certain meaningful messages. We have argued that the development of purposive and effective devices for excluding information as an acquired system of behavior is learned at an early age in the normal human individual.

It would appear, then, that any voluntary muscle whatever (and insofar as we know, any smooth muscle, too) can act as a noise generator. We would assume that each individual could develop his own self-blocking system; that there would be, in general, a great deal of use of the visual system, of the postural system, and of the speech system, but that there would be considerable individual and cultural differences. As shown in the brilliant studies of David Efrón, gesture, posture, stance, and facial expression are cultural devices to invite or drive away social messages, and in these patterns we may pass our defensive lives.

A little Italian village south of Rome, for example, offers very little by way of material goods to its inhabitants, but it offers them a considerable amount of open space, and in their gesticulations their arms sweep through almost the entire sphere around the head. However, the ghetto Jew, living in a crowded, "squeezed" life space, brings hands and elbows close in to the side, a symbolic attempt at defense. The dance, the world of sports, especially the theater, magnify our possibilities of understanding, pulling in and throwing out whole whirlwinds of muscular response, welcoming one idea by pulling it in, rejecting another by tossing it out.

Which muscles are specially relevant to the present approach? Most of these movement systems can be activated or held still in an almost cramplike form for hours at a time. The respiratory system, however, is continuously and more or less rhythmically active. It is of interest that in the disciplined systems of control, such as yoga, breathing has been heavily stressed. It gives a dynamic and continuous expression, more or less in keeping with the intensity of bodily activity, thus maintaining the necessary oxygen supply. But it is closely articulated with the speech system and it may be used for hyper- or hypoventilation, with all its complex biochemical consequences. India has thus magnified and cultivated breath control as a central part of the teaching of yoga.

There are some advantages in working with a system directly involved in the act of defense, as such; a defensive system would be expected to make use of the defensive organs of the body. These, under normal circumstances, are primarily the hands and the arms. Unless artificial weapons of offense and defense are available, men fight with their hands and their arms very much more than with their teeth or their legs. In a world of thrust and parry, childhood fighting turns gradually into the use of sticks, clubs, swords—or stones, or hand grenades—an extension of the primitive defense system. Instrumentally, the hands and arms are accessible to the electronically minded researcher. Robert Malmo used the arm of a patient whose aggressive fantasies directly reflected themselves in the forearm muscles.

Sometimes, however, it is the striped muscular system as a

whole that interests us as a defense system. We begin to see why Sigmund Freud seventy-five years ago hit upon the device of asking his patients to lie on their backs on a couch, so that they would be free to talk without looking into the face of the therapist. Unless the patient goes to sleep, or becomes so agitated that he cannot maintain this supine position, he is well relaxed and somewhat disposed to the reduction of defensiveness with which we are concerned here. But there may be, so to speak, a need to be strenuous in the relaxation process. This strenuousness may show itself from time to time in defensive restlessness, which may nevertheless allow critical memories or attitudes to appear.

The analyst in the meantime is "listening with the third ear," and there is a sort of attunement at the muscle-relaxation level, as free associations, both of patient and of analyst, run their course. In everyday group life, many of us may swing into the same alternations of activity and relaxation and may achieve collective insights through generalized reduction of tension evoked by new viewpoints. The speech of Mark Anthony over the body of Caesar produces not only moments of great excitement but moments of great shared resolution, of almost magical agreement. There is collective self-deception through collective tightening of muscles, but there is also the possibility of collective emancipation. The group insights, as the more astute students of the crowd—and the encounter group—have shown, enable some truths to be grasped in the crowd or group situation, with its casualness and informality, which could never be grasped in an "uptight" social situation.

POSTURAL SET

Many psychologists would describe the foregoing in terms of "postural set." As J. F. Dashiell showed, attention and orientation are partly matters of postural muscle activity. Some would say we know very little about what the postural *muscles* are doing, and would simply describe the phenomena in terms of "set," or preparedness. But it is the muscular aspect of the process of "set" that we are emphasizing here, very much as Dashiell did. "Set" can sharpen or blur; it can pull in or pull out; it can magnify or minimize; it can obliterate or make universal. It is the great physiological factor in the synchronizing of patterns of reality acceptance and reality rejection. "Set" and "ego" are closely related. It is the "set" toward life that we see in the face and posture. The ego is never fully lost, even in panic. And there must remain some primitive individualistic reality-testing mechanisms even while all the "set" functions are patiently at work. The ego will seldom be neutral in respect to the acceptance or rejection of information.

Of course, if one uses physiological concepts when speculating about psychodynamic principles, one may think of the ego as largely a perceptual-cognitive system, relying on brain mechanisms, and not concern oneself with muscles at all. But from the present speculative point of view, it seems likely that the ego thus considered is not only an aspect of brain dynamics but is related to the dynamics of eye-muscle and speech-muscle activity, and indeed probably related to the entire voluntary muscle system. The ego, in other words, is itself involved in the effort; it is itself at a given time either rejecting or rejecting the process of rejecting. If the ego is considered as a formal name for a group of interrelated acts of enhancing and defending the self, it has, of course, emotional as well as perceptual and learning aspects; it is a system of emotion and impulses organized in part for offensive and defensive purposes. It utilizes reality testing and the control of the action system as major components in every effort on behalf of the self. It uses the muscles because it uses everything it has. Additionally, however, the muscles are of major importance not only in momentary battles but also in the continuous lifelong defense of self.

POSITIVE RESPONSE TO REALITY

In Chapter 2 emphasis was placed on the positive response to the environment. Now after looking at acts of defense, we must look again at the positive outgoing response to the world and to the self. All of these acts of defense and offense involve selective awareness, emphasis, figure-ground differentiation, and attention. One of the tasks of attention is to enrich the sensory input; another is to assist in the *integration* of sensory input. When we learn to type, for example, we shift from giving attention to separate letters to the act of attending to the whole word. Once the integration is achieved, it is an integrative system; that is, the organism as a whole is accepting or rejecting a particular percept or thought. Insofar as the environment to which the individual must respond is unified, there must be a corresponding unified response, as grasped in the Gestalt utilization of the term "isomorphism," which in a sense implies brain correspondence to the body stimulus. If the whole organism, and not just the stomach, is hungry, then the pattern of the diner's behavior is not a stomach pattern but an organismic pattern. The organism is, so to speak, drawn into a hunger shape. Robert Levine showed that in the presence of hunger, the shapes of nonsense figures were actually drawn into food shapes. We may go further and say that the individual, insofar as he is dominated by a drive or system of drives, and insofar as he is attending to the relevant means of satisfying that drive or system of drives, is drawn somewhat into an appropriate shape. An enraged man betrays his rage in every trembling finger and in every reddening capillary.

The curiosity motive is no exception here. But it takes an open, free-floating form; the person who is really curious does not insist on deciding what a strange unidentified stimulus must be. He "lets it be itself," as William James said. In the curiosity-driven person, there is a strong urge to avoid standardization of the patterned response; the patterned response must be flexible, so as to fit the outer stimulus pattern. The relaxed musculature is in a literal sense docile, flexible, almost fluid. There is a strong drive to see and to know as well as also a strong drive to be open to whatever is there to be seen or to be known. *Life involves a more or less continuous battle, a struggle toward reality and a struggle against it.*

In a more formal analysis, the essence of feedback, considered in terms of adaptation to the environment, consists of three steps: (1) an uninformed, blind, groping venture into the sensory world; (2) contact with fresh sensory values; (3) modification of response, so that the ensuing behavior is neither the original behavior nor the sheer response to the new sensory material, but a combination or integration of the two. In time, the new material encountered under step 2 can lead to the *anticipation* of step 3. In other words, the first response in the sequence can trigger step 3 without requiring the actual *presence* of step 2. It follows that many stimuli from the outer world can generate "new meanings" based on our action from moment to moment. Messages that come to us as a result of our own action, especially voluntary muscle messages, act to evoke stage 3; stage 3 responses are constantly being regulated by these "proprioceptive" (position and movement awareness) types of feedback. This awareness message, acting jointly with the step 1 process, leads to step 3.

THE INTERACTION OF
BRAIN AND MUSCLE

It has been implicit in our discussion that the brain does not go on continuously with those operations that betoken the process of thinking, while the muscles of the body lie quietly waiting for the brain to tell them to go to work. The intimate unity and reciprocity of brain and muscle appears even during our gentlest musings; changes in bioelectrical voltage are seen darting over the body like the scattered illumination of heat lightning. Learning to pick up these voltage changes, as they accompany the thinking process, has taught the physiologist and the psychiatrist some elementary beginnings of an understanding of the role played by the muscles in shutting out messages that we do not like.

We are constantly taking in and shutting out. As we introduce "noise" into the channel, we become more and more skillful in rejecting unwelcome reality. Later, we can learn what we are doing by feedback skills. We begin to close in on the specific region where the introduction of noise is going on. This often means the identification of the specific muscle-groups involved. There is, so to speak, self-blinding by hands, eyes, tongue, and the breathing apparatus. Sometimes the process seems to be very broadly scattered through the body; one tightens up as a whole bodily system. The generalized rejection of an unwelcome line of thought can be carried out by massive movements of hands and arms as in pushing away: "Don't give me that stuff." Sometimes the tongue and speech apparatus as a whole can do it better; in the symbolic rejection through inner speech, one avoids the symbols that would lead into unwelcome thoughts. The respiratory process is particularly effective because it is semivoluntary—it will go on when you don't think about it—but it is also partly voluntary and you can get good "operant" control over it. The visual system also synchronizes with the speech and respiratory systems. Furthermore, there is in the analytic situation and in most therapeutic situations the isolation of our patient from his personal world, his family, friends, and associates who play similar roles to those that he plays, preventing them from supporting, at the time, his evasion of present or past "unwelcome messages." The organized battle against reality is well played by the group, as many a study of group formation and group action shows. This phenomenon of collective self-deception and conjoint use of the muscles of many in building a wall against vast areas of information has its implications too for therapy: the group can often achieve a therapeutic effect through the synchronization and mutual support of actual muscular systems, including especially the visual, the vocal, and the manual systems used in a collective symbolic battering ram against the wall of rejection. From "encounter groups" to psychoanalytically organized therapy groups, there can be massive rejection of private self-deceits.

In brief, the set to accept or reject information must be not only cortical (a matter of the brain) but also muscular. Set is a matter of the whole psychophysiology of the organized individual. This helps partly to explain how set not only excludes a specific localized message but can also sharpen or blur, pull in or push out, magnify or minimize, obliterate or make universal.

THE SPLIT WITHIN THE SYSTEM

This way of looking at the matter suggests that the overcoming of self-deception literally involves a fundamental conflict, a splitting of the individual straight down from the top to the bottom. There are drive factors, urge factors, or "instinctive" factors, supporting one's deep avoidance of reality, but there also are deep factors of drive, urge, and instinct that push toward an integration through curiosity and the specific practical advantage that will come from getting a better contact with reality. If one thinks of the ego as the relatively rational, practical, organized system for dealing with reality, one can no longer think of a straightforward battle between the ego and the blind forces of animal impulse. On the contrary, as Freud early made clear in *The Ego and the Id*, the ego is not homogeneous; it is divided against itself. There are strong ego factors that say, "Let me alone, I don't want to know any more"; and there are strong ego factors that say, "The time has come to face it."

[77]

The ego cannot be neutral because it is not a unit. It is not a pure ethereal or ideal force acting upon or against the body. The ego system is as much a physiological system as the id or basic drive system; or more accurately, the ego and id working together as part of one organic system are wrenched in a conflict that involves the system of symbols locked in battle— some elements of the ego system and some elements of the unconscious drive system are on one side, the side of self-confrontation, while others are bent upon protecting the secret. The muscles are dependable allies neither of one viewpoint nor of the other; the muscular system is involved on both sides in the fray. Fortunately, the techniques are already available to discover electronically which of the muscle groups are involved in each side of the contest. As Braatoy showed, fighting against painful memories means that both the flexor and the extensor muscles of arms and hands may be involved in a painful conflict. In overcoming self-deception, muscles are powerful enemies but also powerful allies.

THE USE AND MISUSE
OF INFORMATION THEORY

It has become very obvious that information theory has something important to offer in relation to our theme of seeking reality. It is worthwhile to speak of the openness of channels, the differentiation of signal from noise, and the enhancement of the signal-to-noise ratio. A close look, however, at the parallel we encounter here between ordinary human self-deception and the failures of messages to get through channels brings us to a curious blind spot in theory building; indeed, the same blind spot with which self-deception is always concerned, and with which this book is concerned. It is not sheer noise that deafens us. The same loud noise at the same loudness level, and lasting for the same length of time, can be serious or can be trivial, depending upon the significance of the noise for our needs and our ongoing activities. If the noise, let us say, in the form of one's own twisting of one's fingers and gnashing of one's teeth, drumming or pounding or tightening in the pit of the stomach, serves to mute somewhat the awful character of the message, or if the more extreme contortion of muscles can actually prevent the message from being grasped, this is indeed the use of noise to mask the signal, and what will happen will depend upon many factors besides the sheer loudness level. A useful application of information theory will be concerned with the symbolic value of the noise. Above all, the question is how the noise is used by the listener.

Information theory may be mistakenly clothed in an artificial simplicity in which the masking or inhibiting value of noise is treated as a physical dimension for the engineer. The engineer, when confronted with the present thesis, is likely to reply in turn that ours is an artificial complexity; that we have brought the difficulties of personality study into a simple question of communication. This verbal and conceptual battle cannot be won. The real question is rather the question of getting the greatest mileage out of clinical and experimental research that deals with the rejection and exclusion processes and seeing that their implications are grasped and used. In time, information theory will begin to recognize the intricate role that noise plays.

But information seldom bludgeons us into a fresh awareness by attacking and subduing the offending noise. Such awareness as we have is likely to be vague; often it takes the form of "good luck," or "charisma," or "serendipity." It is like the discovery of penicillin, which threw itself suddenly upon a prepared mind, or it takes the form of "eavesdropping," in which we are listening for one bit of gossip, until a very different one, far more exciting, drops in upon us. Sometimes it is the struggle with reality, the wrestling with the angel that enables Jacob to encounter what he never knew was there. The outcome of this struggle for the unknown, according to the book of Genesis was confrontation with the supernatural: "I have seen God face to face, and my life is preserved" (Genesis 32:30). The burden of these tales is that unexpected truth falls upon us suddenly if we are prepared; that is, if the isomorphic readiness for the specific truth is there. This was what the Pythagoreans explored in their secret colony in the south of Italy. They believed that there is an exact hand-in-glove fit between the seeking person and the reality sought. The student of music knows that the tuning of the lyre will give either a fit to reality or a misfit, either of chord or of discord, and however great one's "habituation" to music may be, there is ultimately a need for the nervous system of man to synchronize with many of the rhythmic messages from a vast cosmic system. This has been the theme of a beautiful book by Donald Hatch Andrews, *The Symphony of Life*, a mathematical, physical, chemical basis of that resonance to reality which is harmony.

THE CONTROL OF MUSCLE TENSION

Many of the researchers and clinicians upon whose work we have drawn have emphasized painful, incapacitating tensions, like writer's cramp, and painfully awkward positions while carrying on one's work. The tension often proved to have a large and meaningful "psychological core," in the sense of maintaining awkward and stiff positions as a sort of way of crowding out distracting messages that one does not wish to receive.

We assumed, probably with too much confidence, that the story was fairly simple, and that there were at least two major operations that the defensive subject carries out: (1) a mass blocking effect achieved by activating the whole suit of armor at once, and (2) a more precisely localized and purposefully aimed activation of particular muscles for particular purposes. We thought from clinical studies of local "psychosomatic" and "somatizing" operations that individuals had unwittingly learned how to activate particular muscles to prevent other muscles from getting their messages through to the centers, and we gratefully noted specific evidence like that of Robert Malmo, relating to muscle groups that were particularly active while certain kinds of memories were being explored. We had been studying muscle relaxation techniques and knew of the extraordinary success of Basmajian (repeated in several laboratories) in reducing skeletal muscle "firing" to an absolute flat zero, so that we had high hopes of training our subjects with feedback techniques, both to observe how tight they were as the record showed itself on the wall panel and to relax to the point of obliteration of certain local muscular tensions. We did not know how far this would lead. But Elmer E. Green became confident that one might be able simultaneously to get (a) a desired level of voluntary muscle relaxation, (b) a desired level of involuntary muscle relaxation, (c) voluntary control of the EEG. This might become a method of achieving broad understanding of the nature of "voluntary" control of "involuntary" processes.

Indeed, the voluntary control of the involuntary ("unstriped") musculature—for example, the gastrointestinal canal, or the cardiovascular system—and the control of the heart, as in the work of Malmo and others, suggest the possibility that the feedback concept may thus apply very broadly. The possibility arises that the relaxation concept may apply to the emotional life, the visceral system as a whole. Much work has been done on this in the Soviet Union, and repetitions and elaboration of such studies are beginning to suggest that a great deal could be achieved by voluntary control of organs, hitherto thought to be literally "involuntary."

[81]

N. Miller and his collaborators have shown, for example, how animals can be trained to direct the flow of blood from one organ to another.

These new sources of understanding will probably "fit" well into many older and always needed sources of information about the self: the testimony of others, information coming from conversation, the whole educational process, or the whole psychotherapeutic process. There is no limit to the kinds of information that could be processed with reference to this problem. But quite central is the fact that we cannot achieve much without feedback. It will require a delicate cooperative development, using jointly psychiatric, psychological, and electrophysiological skills, to find the most effective way of revealing to the individual those aspects of self which he is shutting out.

We are usually told—absolutely correctly—that as soon as a person discovers where the bad news comes from he will seal off at that point. That is, a person can always play great games in the art of defending himself. Our reply is very modest and very limited: suppose there should be somewhere, somehow, a scientist who would admit that he probably had a good deal of self-deception in his own scientific work; suppose that such a person does not feel that he is going to be able to find out all of his self-deceptions just by talking to himself, or writing autobiographies, or talking to his psychotherapist, or by any other device. He admits it is going to be a tough struggle, but he thinks that maybe he could get a 10 percent gain, or something worthwhile, if he would go through a process of self-training in which he would begin to generate information about himself that had previously been excluded. His conclusion might be that even if it does not solve all problems, it might be an important step forward in giving him some information in areas where he had not been effectively receiving it.

Now, of course, being rather visionary ourselves, we think

that this will lead beyond what would be useful to only one scientist at one time regarding one issue, but we would settle for that. If we could help one scientist at one time, one place, to reduce by 10 percent, or whatever, the mass of self-deception under which he is staggering, we would still say it is worthwhile.

CHAPTER 7

William James and the Message in the Margin of Awareness

IN ALL LIKELIHOOD, whenever we look away, as in Luborsky's experiment cited on page 56, we vaguely know we are looking away, and when we recapture the visual field, it is because we vaguely want to recapture it. Of course, there *may* be total blindness to one's own total blindness (as when we blink), but it seems likely that there is usually much "double talk," much gamesmanship, much fooling ourselves as to the extent of our self-deception. In fact, we probably all acquire a system of self-to-self signaling; there may be a shakedown ordered in terms of our personal code, so that the tightening of the vocal cords, or drumming of the fingers, or kicking of the toes, really says: "Yes, yes, I know; I just don't want to face it now." Of course, as some signals get too obvious, they may be displaced by others more appropriate to the task. These little personal signals are taken over and internalized in the process of identification with the parents or heroes, or everyday stalwarts on whom we rely. Many of the signals get streamlined so that a single signal in its deft simplicity stands for a whole class of unwelcome ideas which have to be rejected because they stand for something unlovely that is being rejected as a whole. There is always a signal that says something about what is being rejected. Many types of therapy carry us rather quickly from these signals to their old meanings, and a skilled therapist or counselor may find generalized rules of self-deception that appear in the life of each client with monotonous regularity.

Yet all of these little games, skillful and effective though they may be, cannot completely obliterate the basic reality relationships. The world, the task, the duty, the ideal, and the commitment are there. All these devices of evasion are essentially deformations of the shape of the human being. It takes a certain labor to maintain the distorted outlook, whether of the kind that blocks the receipt of the message or of the kind that distorts the message on its way.

But there are built-in modalities of rejection and distortion. It may take hard work to remain as ignorant as we need to be. A little blindness, a little deafness, a little falsification of memory is to be expected. But we men and women in civilized society have enormously added to this machinery; we have elaborately strengthened and built into ourselves higher strategies and modalities for keeping ourselves in a twisted relation to the world, and the twisting process costs us a great deal of hard work—this, in fact, suggests the solution to the tightened muscles, the averted eyes, the production of noise, with which we have been mainly concerned.

It would follow, then, that we could, with suitable skills and suitable application of the known methods of overcoming self-deception, elevate ourselves slowly to a point where we might begin to resonate to the real world and begin to enjoy it far more than we could enjoy the production of acceptable self-images. This is indeed what the training of a scientist or a historian or a logician or a physician or an engineer or a psychologist may actually become. It may be a process by which the tangled, autistic irregularities, noncorrespondences of inner structure to outer pattern, can be drawn into a new harmony, with some hurts in the process but a great deal of inner triumph.

So, by unwitting self-deception we refer both to the deeply and absolutely unconscious part of the mind—if there be such —and also to the vaguely, furtively, coyly, elusively around-the-corner, hide-and-seek quality of "playing games" with ourselves by which we keep the monster waiting for us. This latter calls for much more study here.

It was William James who saw deeply into the problem of this furtive margin of awareness and recognized that our control of our lives depends absolutely upon the operations going on in this half-concealed region. Seldom does a character (like Edmund in *King Lear*) tell all the world that he is a deceiver. Seldom does one (like Iago) develop an explicit creed to support his ignoble soul. For the most part, the elf-like fears of unlovely possibilities, pretending to a virtue that they have not, catch a moment of less rigorous self-control, or there are unstable moments of an ideal self, first pulling a tempting thought into the middle of awareness, then booting it out; one may invite the stern but generous picture of a true and loyal self and give it a moment's genuine hospitality, find no real "resolution," despite the long hours, or years, of preparation, and then lapse back into the safe and sane. What James has especially in mind is a matter of loyalty to a personal goal. It is our own integrity, our honesty, that is at stake. Forever memorable is James's account of an incident in the laboratory in which a physiological demonstration was not going right; the animal would simply not make the reflex response expected of him. James, however, fired by scientific zeal and identifying with the scientific demonstrator, yielded for a moment, fudged the experiment, and supplied the little initiative that the animal had failed to provide. What for a lesser man would have been an overriding experience of "guilt," was—in James's account—a half-solemn, half-humorous mixture of human understanding and human inconsistency, blessed with the telling charm of a moment of utter escape from self-deception.

FROM THE VAGUELY TO THE CLEARLY CONSCIOUS

In the course of James's analysis of the "five types of decision," he leads us to those challenging or inscrutable moments in which there is full, explicit organized mobilization of the self in the decision; and here we find invaluable clues to the processes in which we insist on being aware of much which we ordinarily try to escape. In *Psychology: A Briefer Course,* he states:

In the fifth . . . we feel, in deciding, as if we ourselves by our own willful act inclined the beam. . . . [The] slow dead heave of the will that is felt in these instances makes of them a class altogether different subjectively from all the three preceding classes. . . . Whether it be the dreary resignation for the sake of austere and naked duty of all sorts of rich mundane delights, or whether it be the heavy resolve that of two mutually exclusive trains of future fact, both sweet and good . . . one shall forevermore become impossible, while the other shall become reality, it is a desolate and acrid sort of act, an excursion into a lonesome moral wilderness.

Such passages are often quoted to show how James felt about the freedom of the will. The whole modern impact of James's luminous contribution is in danger of being deflected to this one metaphysical issue of the meaning of freedom, while his rich, beautiful, intensely valuable, and very modern conception of how the will actually operates has been almost wholly forgotten. I believe that there are very few ideas about self-knowledge that are as fundamental and valuable as the working conception that James developed regarding the nature of voluntary processes.

This working conception of James's involves five essential ingredients. First, the conception of effort, the "dead heave of the will." Second, the conception of attention: effort is not devoted originally or primarily to innervation of the muscles but consists rather of the selection, from among the possible ideas that might influence conduct, of one idea rather than a competing idea. We have no voluntary control over the selection of events in immediate awareness; we have voluntary control only over the amount of energy with which we invest each component in immediate awareness. Third, flowing from this, is the conception of attention as moving freely among the contents of consciousness, the transitive as well as the substantive states, identifying one for sanction, approval, executive function, or authorization and pulling it into the center of consciousness. Fourth, *holding* this idea firmly within the structure of the mind. These last-named ideas, about selecting ideas and holding ideas in awareness, have been mentioned rather frequently in current discussions of attention. Of course, in and through all this system of Jamesian suggestions is the *fifth* suggestion, the notion of ideomotor action in which the central idea releases, triggers, and gives life to the waiting muscular system. How many times do we hear today that our theories of learning do not tell us precisely how central functions, whether conceived in cerebral or in ideational terms, actually precipitate motor action! Yes, one reason we do not hear this is that we have forgotten James. The Jamesian fivefold system is a central, rather than a peripheral, theory of the will—an effortful theory, an attentional theory, an ideomotor theory.

It is also a researchable and a testable theory. When Charles Solley and John Santos were working on some problems in attention, they found that voluntary reversal of Necker cubes (See Figure 4) was possible *only* for those subjects who had already experienced spontaneous reversals that had then

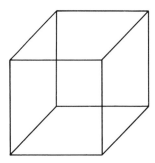

Figure 4. Necker Cube. The cube alternates from
front to back when gazed at steadily.

been reinforced. We all went back through James's chapters
on "Attention" and "Association" and noted leaping at us the
conception that we can give voluntary attention only to that
to which we have already given *in*voluntary attention. The
creative modern experimenter need not be held to the
operant possibilities inherent in James's theory. We only wish
to remind the historically minded student of the evolutionary sequence in James's thinking: there must be a spontaneous
or involuntary movement of attention, in any sense in which
one wishes to formulate attention, leading into one final common path rather than another, *before* there can be that centrally known phenomenon of choice among possible courses
of action. The choice process, the voluntary act of attending,
follows within a network preceded by involuntary attending.

FEEDBACK AND
THE JAMES THEORY

This is the limit we must set upon the earlier historical and
philosophical aspects of our problem. But we are in the midst
of a new, modern chapter: a research approach to the will; a

series of questions about the twentieth-century approach to the processes of thinking, deciding, and willing, as they lead into action—as they pass, Freud would say, from the executive function of the ego to the sphere of motor response. Let us bring the story up to date from 1890, the Jamesian landmark, to our own decade.

One of the great difficulties with the study of the will used to be the sheer fact that the will—whatever it is—could not, until now, be *directly observed*. One obvious reason is that it moves so fast. Another is the fact that we observe what is in consciousness, and not what is below the threshold of consciousness; and there is every reason to believe, from clinical and experimental findings, that the act of will is, to a very considerable degree, controlled by unconscious forces. Even that part of the total array of conscious activity which immediately precedes the decision is literally unobservable, for if the observer is busy watching, he is not busy deciding. If he is involved in the act of willing, this is where his life is invested at the moment, not in an act of observation. We may conclude that the situation is rigged against finding a solution to the problem of the will through utilization of the classic introspective methods of observation.

But we can restate the difficulties in a form more closely akin to the scientific issues of today: first, as far as causes are concerned, they are always multiple—often crisscrossing in space and time, often fusing or blending in higher-order interactions—offering us simple generalizations like the laws of mechanics, but never offering to human perception anything of that order of simplicity. One or another form of the doctrine of flow or plasticity or field relationships or vector dominates the thinking of physics, and likewise the thinking of biologists. From this point of view, factors inside the individual and factors outside the individual are constantly encountering one another in complex, glancing, or fusing interactions. *Concrescence* is the word that Whitehead used—things grow together. Bergson made clear that each act of decision is literally unique and cannot be broken down in terms of some inner components encountering at the moment some outer components in a manner predictable from mathematical equations. Science may be deterministic in the sense of trying to find, to the very last detail, what the context of the new events may be, but it is often the unique interaction with which we have to be concerned.

In respect to the main difficulties—that decision processes move so fast and that they cannot be directly observed as they occur—they will most likely be met by a change of venue, a new stance in which one makes the most of all the knowledge that indicates the intimate dependence of mind, as we know it, and body, as we know it, upon one another. The doctrine of the ultimate oneness of the body-mind reality (as proclaimed by Spinoza), despite the fact that different aspects are being observed at different times, provides a viewpoint from which it is legitimate to study the stream of consciousness by studying the stream of physiological activity in the brain. One must not assign consciousness the trivial role of a mere byproduct or epiphenomenon, but one should note that within the phenomenal world of our daily experience there are laws and orderly recurrences in conscious processes which are intimately related to laws and concurrent events at the physiological level. Indeed, our psychophysiological laboratories are constantly pinpointing exquisite, delicate relationships between conscious activity in relaxed states on the one hand, and brain and muscle activities on the other.

THE USE OF
MODERN INSTRUMENTATION

From this viewpoint, while never becoming dogmatic as to what corresponds ultimately with what, we can find dozens of exciting functional relations between fresh stimulation, perception, imagination, thought, and the setting in which action is precipitated. One may thus work with one's physiological observations right up to the moment of decision, and see how the impending biological climax of an affirmative or a negative decision is actually attained. All that is needed is an instrument with tremendous "gain"—that is, capable of enormously magnifying slight physiological effects so that we can see them spread broadly on a panel; and at the same time, the techniques of slow-motion picture photography by which that which seems to come instantly can be shown to occur over hours or weeks of time. We have all seen photographic studies of the growth of plants and trees in which the year is compressed into a minute. We can likewise see on the panel the development of a complex of tension patterns which precede the massive thrust of a new movement. We can, at the same time, feed back to the individual a little knowledge of what his brain and his muscles are doing. He can watch, as he decides, again and again, how his earlier decision processes were registered and, indeed, where they came from. There is no chance that any individual could see all this without the requisite instrumentation any more than he could see bacteria without a microscope, or a remote galactic system without a telescope, or analyze blood without biochemistry, or look at the finely localized functions within the brain without implanted electrodes.

But we have all these tools, and more are being invented, and they call loudly to us to use them. How very different things look when we observe them with modern instruments! The apparently instantaneous character of a flash of thought led the eighteenth-century poet, William Cowper, to write: "How fleet is a glance of the mind! / Compared with the speed of its flight / The tempest itself lags behind, / And the swift-winged arrows of light." No such thing, we say. Wilhelm Wundt measured reaction time in Leipzig in 1880, and from reaction to simple stimulation there follow reactions to very complex materials among which decisions and discriminations must be made. Precision in time measurement was not at first possible for complex processes, but this is exactly the kind of thing that is now becoming possible.

In our laboratories today the sequence of psychological events that differentiates the response to stimulation of 1/1,000 of a second from response to 30/1,000 of a second is a part of Howard Shevrin's study of subliminal processes. Shevrin has not begun to use slow-motion pictures, nor does he need to yet. The student of the will, however, needs only to watch on his panel and on his sensitive paper the temporal flow of the processes that lead toward the climax of will, those shifts in muscle tension that even crude observation reveals to us in eye, neck, and hand, in pulse, breathing, and blood pressure. We are suggesting that simplification is often a prime step in science, and that removal of confusion in the observation of space and time units is central to accurate observation. Indeed, for some years now neurophysiologists have been using instruments known as "computers of average transients," which filter out disturbing rhythms to make some hidden rhythm more observable. It has been evident in psychoanalytic psychology that there are many components of the ego, and indeed of the superego as well, and that a good many of them are ready for physiological observation.

CENTERING IN THE WILL

William James may have been right in thinking that an act of will consists of putting some effort into the process of taking hold of some marginal impression in the mind, some little suggested possibility of action, and, with unified effort, pulling this vague—perhaps unnamed or even repugnant—thought out there in the margin of the mind into the center, where, when once attended to, it can precipitate action, triggering into being the full-fledged bodily expression of a decision. From this viewpoint the will would be an inner process rooted in the fact of attention. In fact, voluntary attention would be a centrally initiated—or, if you like, ego-controlled—act of attending to one thing and of non-attending to all which compete with it. Since acts of attention are already yielding, in many laboratories, to some experimental and psychophysiological analysis, there is no a priori reason why we might not soon hope to see exactly those effortful acts of attending that James described and look at them, so to speak, with a psychological microscope, that is, through instruments with sufficient gain to permit the free examination of the time-space pattern. At the same time we would be investigating the threshold dynamics, those factors which determine whether an impression can get over the threshold and appear in conscious life or must remain unconscious. We might go on to study the ways in which the threshold is itself manipulated by the impulse system—that is, making oneself more sensitive to certain types of activities in the environment, more ready to observe them, and less ready to observe those that compete with them. Ego and superego would become, from the psychophysiological point of view, devices for making some things more clearly observable and others less so.

Of course when we consider the whole array of possible acts and systematically direct our attention to the consequences of a particular line of action, we may then begin to ask what the converging forces, the systematic field relationships of the observer at the time, are contributing. Here there would certainly appear that great central function of unified action that William McDougall called the "self-regarding sentiment," the system of ideas related to acceptance, pride, and respect of one's own self-image, as contrasted with self-disparagement and self-hate. The system of forces at work in many decisions would probably be those related to some hope of appearing well both in the eyes of others and in one's own eyes, weighing such various consequences against the stress and effort needed to implement the decision and the risk of being misunderstood, together with all the other personal and social factors that weigh against the decision.

It is quite possible that the individual can inform us, after a decision is made, about many of the steps that preceded that decision, particularly if he has been trained by feedback methods to recognize subtle forces constantly going on as the decision takes shape. But it is quite likely that he will have to *learn* to observe, being trained step by step through observation of the panel. We know from the work of D. Aserinsky, N. Kleitman, and W. Dement, and many others, that the individual, awakened at the appropriate moment when he is showing rapid eye movements, may give a fuller and more adequate account of a dream than one who has slept through the night, done a half-day's work, and has made his way to the psychoanalytic couch. We have no interest in making any guesses regarding the therapeutic values and significances here. We are concerned solely with the suggestion that instruments may help us to know ourselves, and certainly not only in connection with our perceiving, remembering, and thinking but also with reference to our willing.

It may be assumed by some of our readers that we are, as it were, "closing in" upon the will, and that we have every hope that it can be trapped in a corner and fully disposed of. *No;* that is far, far away from the way the issue looks today. Let us consider what will probably happen. With a burst of new information obtained by using the new methods at hand, we may rapidly increase our competence in predicting the pre-decision and decision processes. It does not follow, however, that we shall reach the same level of satisfactory prediction found, for example, in the more exact portion of the world of physiology. It is just as likely that the relationships we are studying will be asymptotic; that is, we shall find ourselves approaching a limit, which is actually not full prediction but a point considerably below that. There may be much noise in the system; there may be much inherent inefficiency that will cause a substantial gap, say à la Heisenberg's principle of uncertainty, so that even with our best efforts we shall reach only a realm of unknown significance to us, perhaps removable by later instrumentation or conceptualization, but perhaps not.

The other possibility remaining is that, as Erwin Schrödinger has suggested, we may be dealing not with smooth curves of the sort we have suggested but with step functions, or sudden jumps. It may be that we can, at certain moments, jump from one level to another. If the jumps grow smaller and smaller, it may be that a jump will never occur that will carry us over the last gap, as in hitting the last stake in croquet and "going out." But in view of the modesty of the scientific enterprise, as suggested in the uncertainty principle, it may well be that we shall never know whether there is a last jump coming or whether, in all eternity, it is more reasonable simply to rule it out. We must not make the common assumption that Heisenberg's principle has something to do with some principle of ultimate chance, the Greek *tyche*, the ultimate unresolvable last trump of the universe in its game with us. We are saying rather that there is simply no way of knowing, with our present conceptual and instrumental tools, whether there is a gap between the knowable on the one hand and the realm of complete prediction on the other. For the present, this question need not even arise. If we use the conceptual and instrumental devices of today, we have reason to believe that we shall close in on the will in quite a different sense—namely, that we shall be able to state more and more clearly what the various components in a voluntary decision are, particularly the components related to the structure of ego and superego.

THE WORLD OF CONFLICT

But we have still left out the issue of smoothly rolling function versus bound energies, blockage, inhibition—in short, the world of conflict. If there is one force that suggests the possible fulfillment of a need of whatever sort, and if there are no countervailing factors, we would expect that the early phases of the decision would run smoothly and rapidly and that we should then find ourselves having done what we wanted to do. We may be caught in conflict between two more or less equally desirable *goods*, or we may have to choose one rather than the other of two alternative *evils*. The will, however, is always an expression of alternatives in which something must be given up, or a pain accepted as a way to avoid another pain or to achieve a positive goal. One primitive form of the will, indeed, can be demonstrated even in very lowly animals, which turn from one to another goal, as in the delightful image of the "schematic sowbug" described by Edward Tolman, which predictably swings toward one goal until, after a moment's satiation, it must swing to the competing goal. Norman Maier conducted a series of experiments with animals in forced choice situations, where, finally confused as to where the food lay, they stood on their little table and swept their eyes right and left for a long time in "vicarious trial and error," or VTE, as Tolman called it. It was not necessary for the rat to scamper. It was only necessary that he use the little "cognitive map" comprising the options and then either finally enter the correct window to reach the food or, if still unsure, continue "V-T-E-ing" for many minutes.

From this viewpoint it is interesting to try to use the language of information theory and the engineering situations that information theory strives to clarify. Information theory would say: "Your trouble is that there is too much noise in the channel." In other words, the conflict situation that we have just described involves coercive and restraining forces —it is quite complex in the rat, and in man, full of symbolic distractions and threats. But the problem is not simply noise, nor is it lack of information. The problem is overload, overcrowding of the channels. One reason why the will is so bumbling and inefficient is the sheer complexity of human beings' innate and acquired needs, their symbols, and values. Don't you feel like Little Jack Horner, proudly extracting the plum, when you have done a long, hard job of driving in difficult traffic, making lots of decisions, and finally coming to port in the garage after a day without an accident? What wears us out is the process of making decisions—one more reason why the will is the whipping boy, the nasty stinging creature from Pandora's box that can never let us alone, for the simple reason that we are a hodgepodge of conflicting responses to multicolored doorways.

OVERLOAD IN THE CHANNEL

The man who had to choose between the lady and the tiger found it hard because he had no basis for a decision, while we who are overloaded with thousands of significant symbolic bases for decision are confronted with an even worse situation. Indeed, even if all the goals are good, there still is a multiple overload in the channel. No wonder, we note, that there is more neurotic strain today than in our grandparents' time. We may die of a surfeit of things, all of them good, among which we must choose. It is not only a prince making a life-and-death decision who cries out against a choice that, as Hamlet says, "puzzles the will." A supermarket, a toy shop, a reading list, an ice-cream store, or a Sears Roebuck catalogue can grind us down by puzzling the will, too.

Many of these decisions are trivial—belonging, as Heinz Hartmann would say, to "conflict-free ego spheres," where the issues are what they seem to be. Often, however, an apparently trivial decision precipitates a moment of self-hate, or a family quarrel, and it becomes obvious that the "trivialities" of the moment are really representatives of awesome moral issues that lurk behind. The decision to face reality is constantly entering into many other decisions, limited or awesome. Indeed it becomes obvious that ego and superego functions stand guard behind the facade of a moment's idle insouciance. Almost all of psychology and almost all of ethics can be marshaled behind a decision to face or to retreat. It may come through a thought, or through an act. After Sir Arthur Sullivan's fingers had traveled over the noisy keys, there came, apparently from nowhere, "the sound of a great amen." From the sublime to the ridiculous, we may say, as we look at the slips of speech, the errors of expression, sprinkled through Freud's *Psychopathology of Everyday Life*. We will honor our host, but actually say that we hiccup his health, or pray not for our dear old Queen, but for our queer old Dean. We meant, we *willed*, one thing, and did another. Shades of Saint Paul: The evil that we would not, *that* we do!

As with James, the vast battle arena of human impulse and human conflict lies open to observation in the split second of an intentional—or unintentional—act. If experimental, physiological, and instrumental modalities of observing can now be added to these clinical observations, we may hope to understand, a shade better than we do today, how the mighty forces of a cultural tradition, the deep intimacies of a personal life, and the subtle inwardness of a struggle among goals, may all be observed a little better and understood a little more clearly than before. Ethical theory, with its concern for the realization of man's fullest potentials, would stand to gain by every clinical and every experimental addition to an understanding of the moment of decision. And James's analysis of the process of choosing—as in the choice whether to face our inner reality or not—will go with us all into the jungles of our decisive moments.

CHAPTER 8

Everyday Ways of Coping with Self-Deception

MOST PEOPLE have little games to correct their biases. These little games serve a useful purpose in reducing stress. Skillful and effective though they often may be, they seldom obliterate the basic trouble. The world, the task, the basic life commitments remain. Insofar as they perpetuate serious deformations in the shape of man, they prevent the utilization of more effective help from friend and from community. Often it takes a certain effort to maintain the distorted outlook, whether of the kind that blocks the receipt of the message or of the kind that distorts the message on its way. But it takes even more effort to give it up, for it is organized in depth.

We have argued that men and women may in time learn to live relatively undeceived—that is, in an undeceived relation to the world. If this is true, the more lucid relationship of the perceiving individual to the world may be duplicated at the level of one's own internal organization; what one perceives within oneself may be as fully cleared of deceit as the perceiver's relation to the outer world is. This is "programmatic," but movement in this direction has been going forward a very long time and is now moving forward at an accelerated rate. The understanding of the world through the physical sciences has been increasing with us since the time of Galileo, some three hundred years ago. Perhaps we are entering upon an era in which there may be a fuller use of the devices by which man's distorted vision of himself can be set right. At least we may describe these devices— however crude and incomplete the list must be—and consider what promise they offer.

1. The first and most obvious weapon to use against self-deception is sheer *fiat;* a determination to put an end to it. Man deceives himself, it has been said, because he is an ornery creature and the truth is not in him, or because woman led him astray, or because, as Saint Ignatius Loyola pointed out, he is forever on a quest for material goods, power, or prestige—*ergo* let him fling the bad habit away. From this viewpoint, it is assumed that man normally sees life and himself essentially as they are, and that self-deception is an occasional fluke, a "missing-the-mark," a sin or natural depravity. There are, so to speak, capsules of truth for the asking, wise precepts, which, taken one at a time, will keep us on the path. But if the process is built in, how rare is the successful moment of self-conquest!

2. Often man's best hope of rectitude is to *oppose his own bias,* nicely attuning and upgrading the lighter tread on the left foot to one's natural heavy-footedness on the right; or, like the man lost in the woods, knowing that he is in danger of walking in a circle, compensating by striding a little further with his weaker foot. Man believes that he can "compensate for his error" or even "lean over backwards." Or when the biases of one man may be overcome by calling in the counterbiases of others, "in the multitude of counselors there is safety," then each oddball will be lost in the mainstream of truth. But this again ignores the depth, the invisibility, the essential unreachability of most built-in biases. The color-blind or "color weak" man cannot overuse his blues and yellows to make up his deficits in reds and greens. Nor can the Beethoven-mad music lover "de-Beethovenize" his view of the world so as to make up for his tone deafness for Chopin or Tchaikovsky or Bartok. Biases are not likely to push steadily in the same direction, nor do they move at constant velocities. One

could lean over backwards well enough if one had a constant error in the direction of leaning one inch forward, but the marksman on the archery range cannot make himself a Robin Hood by aiming each arrow in a direction nicely adjusted to balance his own constant error. How easy life would be if the leaning-over-backwards technique were sound, or if one biased man could be balanced against another "counterbiased" man. This method of "compensation" probably works a little better if one is conscious and keeps some sense of proportion. As the quip goes, "Leaning over backwards is fine as long as you don't bang your head against the floor." The method does not tell how to guide the process, when to stop, or how to recover from the resulting self-inflicted wounds, self-righteousness, and, at the same time, self-hate, which are all likely to follow. John Dewey remarked that a man may make a New Year's resolution to give up slouching and begin to stand up straight, but this inner process of making a promise to oneself has almost no relation to the actual day-by-day control of posture; one literally does not "know how to stand up straight."

3. Almost equally futile, although occasionally helpful in its own way, is the process of "*intellectualizing,*" or getting names for one's "bad habits," or making a self-righteous show of "understanding oneself." This is indeed one of the primary hazards likely to occur with the feedback techniques described in this volume. The point is that one has to see *and feel* oneself in the process. Seeing oneself is not enough. Feedback must be at all psychophysiological levels at which the original difficulty appears. This will mean that the "quick and easy" solutions will usually be failures; it is those that involve full confrontation of the self in relation to a larger goal of self-understanding that are more likely to make at least a fair beginning. On Mount Washington, the ascent may be easy or difficult. There is the Carriage Road for those who want to take it easy, and there is the Nelson Crag trail or the Huntington Ravine trail for those who want to take the mountain by storm.

4. Another method of reducing self-deception involves *confrontation with ourselves in the mirror* or by playback from a sound-recording instrument, preferably with a little chitchat or as much as we can take at any given moment. Honest appraisal can release a flood of emotions and anxiety, when this begins to work. Most of us now have had the experience of hearing our own recorded voices. To hear what we sound like almost always comes as a shock. A simpler way to elicit the same result is to stand

a few inches from a corner wall, and speak into it, so that both ears can hear the words. A more complex result arises from motion pictures or videotapes of our actions and words, with views of our attitudes, manners, gestures, interpersonal positions, and movements. Although the mirror or sound track can be upsetting, such a view can occasionally prove profoundly insightful. In all these instances, modern technology can provide multidimensional mirrors into the functioning personality.

5. Another easy way to see what one has never seen before is to *have others tell us about things from which they ordinarily shield us.* Twice in a thirty-year teaching career, I have been photographed from behind while at the blackboard; and while others enjoyed the snapshots, I did not regard them as "good pictures." This was what Robert Burns was talking about: "O wad some power, the giftie gi'e us / To see ourselves as others see us." But who really wants to see himself as others see him? Perish the thought! One grudgingly learns a little, but how little!

But it is time now to look at a few of the more systematic escapes from self-deception that have been attempted.

6. There is a very intricate system of *evidence testing,* which the legal world has created and which can also be used to reduce self-deception. The difficulty here is first to permit the evidence and then to assess it objectively. How many of us have opinions that would not stand up in court? Opinions about ourselves are often even more thinly based, since our evidence-testing about self is grossly inadequate.

A good variant of this is to write our own obituary, from two points of view: that of a close friend and that of our worst enemy. The friend's views are familiar, but the enemy's would also prove valuable. Here evidence of failures should be carefully stacked up against successes.

7. There is Aristotle's *logic* which has often been used to reach greater self-understanding. Check your reasoning against his syllogism:

> All men are mortal
> Socrates is a man
> Therefore Socrates is a mortal.

Such a check should include a detailed list of formal errors in reasoning. The check should especially seek contradictions, inconsistencies, views subject to change without notice, submission to the views of others, and views based on convenience, fear, and concern for the consequences of one's ideas and actions.

8. Francis Bacon's *inductive scientific method* provides yet another means to gain self-knowledge. We can draw conclusions from many observed cases. John Stuart Mill's laws of inductive inference are related to this process. These both may require historical comparison of past personal events, a task many would find distasteful.

Curiously, this is difficult for scientists, since they are generally willing to use scientific methods in their work but not in their nonworking lives. A diary is extremely helpful with this technique, since it provides more objective evidence of one's past attitudes and incidents, somewhat detached from that most undependable bank, memory.

9. Another device is Darwin's superb method of *keeping notes of phenomena that went contrary to his own theory* (see page xiv). This, of course, is the opposite of what most of us do in daily life. It shares some of the qualities of the obituary written by one's leading opponent. Important for rapid personal growth, it compels a continual questioning of one's most cherished prejudices and preconceptions. At interim steps, it can produce immobilization, and hesitancy, but these may lead to periods of surprising expansion of knowledge and understanding of self.

10. Magnificent indeed was *Freud's systematic study of the mechanisms of defense.* The exploration of the vast realm known as "the unconscious" works largely in the service of the discovery of defensive operations. So profound was Freud's perception that he began to see that the ego was divided against itself, some aspects of the ego being involved in trying to sort out the disguises of other ego aspects. It is indeed largely through the concept of defense, mostly in the sense of exclusion of ideas and emotions, that the psychoanalytic approach has become genuinely comprehensive and systematic.

In its architectural complexity and its architectural wholeness, Freudian psychoanalysis offers amazing vistas. As in a Gothic cathedral, one finds endless rich details of nave, transept, chapel, and altar. The dim light allows us to see much that is unclear even to the adapted eye, and the pattern grows with experience, in the sense that we see new works of art and new complexities of structure on repeated visits. The psychoanalytic method of taking, as it comes, whatever is available to observation in a noncensoring manner offers great possibilities through feedback which are only beginning to be grasped.

I found in my own brief bout (one year) with Freudian psychoanalysis that I had very considerable skill in verbalizing what was wrong with me, not only making some acceptable guesses regarding conscious gamesmanship but also making fairly uncanny guesses regarding the inscrutable and unknowable, and winning my analyst's acceptance. Indeed, I seemed to see some realities head on. But I did not see them in a way that would permit other related realities to be thrown into clear light. It was possible to win, day by day, a number of verbal victories over personal self-deception without altering the essential contours of my own personal bias system. At least, I think that is what was involved.

The necessary principle of "working through" involves *refeeling* each memory and current attitude in relation to all other remembered or confronted feelings and judgments that require a new perspective, at the level of reliving stressful realities. Judging by the experience of some "well-analyzed people," it has a considerable likelihood of enlarging and deepening the scope of self-understanding.

11. *Integrations of analytic thinking with feedback thinking* as by Perls, Hefferline, and Goodman (see page 69) already offer great promise in reducing self-deception. They have developed a model for a kind of internal scanning in which one point after another within the patient's body is explored, with the benefit of Hefferline's psychophysiological skills, thus permitting the "subjective" world of the patient to be mapped and brought into relation to the "objective" world of instrumentation.

12. The *analytic psychology of Jung* can in some respects claim to go further in reducing self-deception, because analysis is never limited to the exploration of conflicts and the modalities of their resolution but, in an open-ended fashion, looks for limitless new potentials of a sort not yet ready to be catalogued by the objective science of today. Instead of leading back to infantile episodes conceived to be the sources of individual pathology, Jung seeks to confront and to deal constructively with a virtually infinite sea of individual and racial memories, fluid and creative; the aim is not to cure a neurosis but to offer help in a widening quest for individual fulfillment. Human "types" comprise not only the familiar extravert and introvert, for much finer differentiations are made. Analysis lays bare a gradually unfolding system, really

concerned less with self-defense than with a release of unguessed potentialities; errors in self-perception fade in the light of discovery of a new person.

13. *The client-centered therapy* of Carl Rogers can create a more solid base of self-understanding. It emphasizes total acceptance of the client and a continuous effort to help him to accept himself, the therapist, the specific situation and life as a whole. Aimed at helping the client to accept life's perspectives as a whole, and to accept himself in this context, it may be the gentlest method, partly because it is the least constraining approach. Perhaps this is one of the reasons why this therapeutic system has tended, in recent years, to become "encounter-centered." The emphasis has shifted to the form or pattern of interpersonal relations in groups and to the feelings of each member of the group toward the others, as well as to the leader, which makes the experimental social group a microcosm of the social macrocosm of which the patient is a member.

14. The psychological systems of Asia, notably *Zen and Yoga,* presently being integrated into Western analytic thinking and supplemented with feedback research techniques, offer an immediate future that is rich with unguessed possibilities. Yoga is an ancient system of self-discipline involving a long and arduous period of practiced and supervised exercises and postures, designed to draw the body and the mind into a serene, passionless preparation for meditation. Some forms of yoga (Hatha yoga) involve extreme, even violent, assault upon the body. Far more important from a Western viewpoint is the rhythmic, contemplative weaning of the person from all interim preoccupations; even fifteen minutes a day of gentle cultivation of appropriate postures may be an important spiritual exercise for millions of Hindus. Such exercises are plainly important for any "humanistic" self-discipline.

Much the same may be said for Buddhist study and exercise of body and mind, especially in the form rapidly becoming widely known in the West. This is the cultivation of the higher level of discipline known to Zen Buddhists as "satori," in which the individual is utterly fused into the universe. But we must not pretend that a few hours or weeks will ever permit miracles.

15. Another method of reducing self-deception is based on Harry Stack Sullivan's principle of *"consensual validation."* One refers each impression to a *confrontation with all other impressions,*

from the senses or from memory and judgment and admits to one's personal courtroom all evidence that can be recognized. At its best this becomes "cognitive therapy"; we park and read the map. There is no magical guarantee that all existing evidence *will* be caught and brought to the courtroom. But at least this method is better than excluding those whose credentials show them to be hostile to the major witnesses. The reality-seeking patient must, with his therapist's help, find validation that is consensual in this extended sense.

16. Self-deception cannot occur without a masking process; and the mask, if not visible from one vista, can always be glimpsed from another viewpoint, provided that the necessary telescope, spectroscope, microscope, reduction screen, and so forth, can be found. Herein lies the supreme value of the theater as a means of revealing self-deception, whether in its classic form or in the form of *J. L. Moreno's "psychodrama."* When viewing a theatrical production, one sees oneself, in a way, in *all* characters. Psychodrama likewise places the group interaction process upon a stage for observation. It involves role-playing in which each actor on the stage—and indeed each spectator in the hall—works through, feels through, participates in, the life approach and life difficulties of that person whose difficulties are made real as well as all persons interacting with them, considered conjointly or in series. As with Aristotle, the ventilation and removal of overpowering feelings through "catharsis" enables the therapy group to confront a blocked emotion and thereby speed up the insight process.

17. *Excluding the exclusion process* also may be used to help us see clearly. Sheer self-alerting to pitfalls, according to our present thesis, indicates that the internal bell that rings when we are deceiving ourselves is really ringing, in some measure, *all the time.* Moreover, there is a jangle of *many* bells ringing in their own cadences over their half-structured cacophony all the time. How *could* it ever stop ringing? Life is a battle for and against information, as walking is at first a battle to advance with the left foot, and to advance with the right foot. Only by each one's successively yielding to the other can either one move at all. The exclusion process is universal. What we must learn is under what conditions one may wisely exclude the exclusion process. Thus we shall have to learn to read not the body language of others but of our own selves. This implies learning to recognize the inhaled breath, when we are ready to strike out verbally; the

muscle tension involved in both getting ready to move and in freezing that movement; the various tics, twitches, and compulsive movements of which we are normally unaware.

18. *Ukhtomsky's dominance principle* tells us that of two action systems invoked simultaneously, the winning one tends ultimately to absorb the energies of the losing one. Although we add new responses we do not multiply indefinitely the number of responses that we then exhibit throughout life. We must drop many responses, while we add a few. We drop them in an orderly way. The strength of the original unconditioned response determines what can be attached to our repertory. If our devotion to a goal, such as confronting reality, is intense, any behavior, however trivial, that assists our progress towards it will become part of our behavioral system. The principle of dominance implies, moreover, that we will lose only those responses which are relatively unimportant, and therefore, that we shall *not* lose the gratifying modes of self-deception through the sheer principle of extinction or disuse.

19. It may be suggested that a way to drive out a comforting habit of self-deception is to make this habit compete with another that involves a more direct confrontation with reality. This conception has interested a great many investigators of the education process, who have been interested in teaching *open-mindedness* or the recognition and removal of prejudice. It began with Goodwin B. Watson's *Measurement of Fair-mindedness* (1925), in which a broad overall pleasure in the process of outgrowing distortion in thinking was achieved. Classroom studies at the high-school and college level were undertaken that pointed out to students their fallacious reasoning. The students, consequently managed to reduce their prejudice scores. Then came a demonstration of a true transfer effect: those who had undergone successful training with one subject matter showed in a new situation (with a new subject matter) a tendency to be on their guard against prejudiced thinking and to avoid it. William W. Biddle demonstrated that acquired skill in recognizing propaganda pertaining to the foreign policy of the United States within one region had some transfer value for recognizing propaganda about other regions, even when there was no overlap in content. Biddle specifically noted, however, that only those students made the transfer who had become aware of the propaganda principles that were being used.

20. This leads, then, to another principle beyond that of sheer dominance—namely, *understanding the distortion going on in the proc-*

ess. It is not just a question of cognitive therapy, facing the objective realities more and more thoroughly, but a question of seeing into one's own dynamics.

Let us look closely at this principle of understanding. What is it that has to be understood? The fact that we are being deceived? This will hardly suffice. We could say, "Well, yes, there's plenty of deceit in life, so what? How is the principle of understanding useful? When is it important enough to goad us into a fresh effort to throw off the deceit?"

21. R. H. Thouless introduced the study of *straight and crooked thinking*, which helps us to see that understanding is effective insofar as we grasp that our self-image becomes worthy or unworthy. If one comes to realize that he is a shoddy thinker—specifically, that what he is doing is accepting cheap and easy solutions rather than searching for the most comprehensive truths that can be achieved—he is essentially (if he values straight thinking at all) recognizing himself as one who has really assimilated such a value. Thus another principle that holds out the promise of reducing self-deception involves the goal of obtaining gratification with one's own picture of oneself as a "straight thinker."

22. Curiosity itself helps to reduce self-deception. We have seen that there is sometimes a genuine delight in seeing *clearly*—a genuine *creative curiosity*, a love of direct contact with reality. True curiosity implies a willingness to approach the world with the child's eyes, ears, hands; to explore feeling and perception anew; to sense what fur really is like, what sound means, how flowers truly smell; how animals and people relate and respond to each other; and finally, to see others as if for the first time, with a willingness to be open to the hurts and joys of early experience.

23. It may seem at first glance that the curiosity approach is closely related to the "*sensitivity training*" and "*encounter group*" methods developed in the past few years. These newer methods offer much in the way of self-discovery, and discovery of the mutuality of two persons and of the many members of both small and large groups. However, it is too soon to predict exactly what will come from the mushrooming proliferation of these new procedures; certainly the shock effect of directly discovering much about one's own body and the bodies of others and the habits of plain speech and of direct emotional expression offer serious scientific possibilities.

It is equally evident, however, that the new ways of thinking and feeling have been moving so fast—without much control or discipline—that they have not yielded firm data or clear followups. They may do wonders for one individual, but may increase the hazard of a psychosis or suicide for another. On balance, they cannot be adequately evaluated even by those who use them unless more rigorously scientific methods are employed. It can be said, however, from the present viewpoint, that they involve feedback to a significant degree; one receives information about oneself in certain kinds of sensitivity and encounter situations, and this must certainly be admitted to be an important form of feedback. One learns, moreover, much about one's own bodily properties as apprehended visually, auditorily, tactually, and above all, through the organic, and especially the visceral, messages. If certain instruments are used properly, the visceral components and the skeletal-muscle component can enlarge the scope of present methods. For example, the encounter-group therapist or the sensitivity-training therapist may familiarize himself with and obtain disciplined training in the various feedback skills, while at the same time those working mainly with proprioceptive feedback may learn how to articulate their methods with the encounter and sensitivity methods. So we have come full circle, to the position we took in Chapters 5 and 6.

A COMPARISON OF METHODS

If our reasoning is correct, successful therapy is essentially a form of biofeedback, involving a new apprehension of reality. Perhaps the time has come to offer the record of a simple process of learning to encounter reality and to see how it can be understood in the terms presented here: a bare narrative of a therapeutic session shows something of what went on. Take the classic study in which Mary Cover Jones undertook to free a small child from his irrational fears. She tried some of the timeworn procedures that humanity has always used, but she also tried some new ones. From her report—written in the early days of the conditioning approach—we learn that she tried at least seven ways of freeing the child of his fear of a rabbit. Here we are taking the liberty of retelling the story in our own words, rearranging and rephrasing the essence of the various methods.*

A. *Habituation.* "Let him alone, don't make an issue out of it, give him time, he'll be all right." No results from this method.

B. *Imitation.* "Let Jack play with Jim; Jim is not afraid of rabbits. Let him get used to the situation of seeing Jim's cool unconcern, and he will come along too." Some slight results by this method.

C. *Verbal directions.* "Talk him out of it." Explain that the rabbit is small and harmless: "He's more afraid of you than you are of him." Some slight results by this method.

D. *Add a peremptory word; a command.* "Stop that, Jack, just cut it out." No results by this method.

E. *Shame.* "That's just too silly. A big boy like you, afraid of a rabbit! You ought to be ashamed of yourself." No results by this method.

F. *Add a number of cognitive redefinitions of the situation.* "Look, Jack. See, he eats lettuce and carrots, not fingers. He wants to play; he doesn't want to hurt you." We don't know how far this could have been pushed with Jack. We do know that successes are claimed by cognitive redefinitions of the situation at many levels and with many varieties of technique.

G. *Counterconditioning.* Whenever Jack was hungry, a snack was given to him, and the rabbit was brought to a point several feet away. The rabbit became a part of the total snack-time situation. Then from time to time, the rabbit was brought nearer at snack time. Ukhtomsky's dominance principle was effectively used. The food-and-gratification situation—safe, swift, and dependable—was regularly used to introduce the experience with the rabbit. The rabbit, being nondominant, took on the attributes of the dominant situation —the snack. There was positive, outgoing satisfaction, in-

* Mary Cover Jones tells me that I have not distorted the story.

cluding vegetative responses, such as salivation, and general relaxation. Eventually Jack lost his fear.

Generally, we may conclude that there are three situations under which this essentially successful model will not work: (1) the child is not hungry, (2) the food is not appetizing, (3) the animal is close enough to evoke fear. If any of these situations, or any combination of them, appears, the dominance relations are reversed, and the child begins to fear his food. It is granted that these steps have not all been worked out with adequate experimental and quantitative control. But the principle of dominance in the counterconditioning situation appears clear. Incidentally, it is, to some degree, a cognitive method, as well, since the relation of the appetizing snack to the appeasement of hunger is clear, and since the rabbit is perceived to be safely sequestered by the attendant at the doorway and not a part of a recurrent threat situation.

It seems fair then to generalize that at the primitive level of analysis offered so far the series of fear-removing techniques for a primitive conditioned fear are all likely to fail, except for the counterconditioning pattern based on the successful use of dominance relationships. The principle is used by modern behavior therapy. But behavior therapy also uses a much more complex system of ideas and techniques.

Jones's work was conceived in Pavlovian (Watsonian) terms; "classical conditioning" was used. From a contemporary viewpoint the grownup experimenters were obviously learning in this situation by operant or instrumental conditioning; they were finding out what worked with Jack and responding to successful "primary reinforcement." Jack was not allowed very much freedom to experiment with his environment in this situation. Although there may have been a good deal of operant conditioning going on (on the part of the rabbit, Jack, and the experimenters), the records are not offered us in these terms. We could quite properly, however, write a brief supplement to the Jones experiment, which would run somewhat as follows:

Jack discovered that putting up a great ruckus in the presence of the rabbit managed to get the grownups to leave the rabbit out of the game from that time forth. (He could have gotten them to substitute toy rabbits, which were biteless, or picture rabbits, which could be torn, or to use small animals like turtles, which from Jack's experience were harmless.) In the present form of the experiment, Jack got the grownups to bring the rabbit to the right spot at the right time, adding to the reinforcing qualities of snack time.

But we can get a great deal more mileage out of Mary Jones's experiment than is obvious at first glance. She used the excellent "dominance principle" of Ukhtomsky and a gradual reduction of resistance, but she also used suggestions from both Gestalt, or holistic, therapy and some behavior-modification techniques. This system of ideas can in turn be developed into a rich form of self-awareness training, in which the whole body with all its messages, one's whole past, one's whole reputation, one's whole system of hopes, and purposes, may be examined individually and in patterns. One develops a good image of oneself, enriching it step by step, either alone or with friends' or therapists' help.

Often today one regards the term "self-image" as a little one-sided, because it deals too much with one's sheer appearance, particularly to visual observation. This deficit is made good by replacing the term "self-image" by the term "self-concept." Self-concept comprises all that one appears to himself to be, whether sensory, imaginal, emotional, conceptual, or what not. Again, the self-concept is what this present approach is asking us to study. We have been urging, however, and must here urge particularly strongly, that the sheer decision to study one's own self-concept cannot possibly accomplish the task. There are too many barriers, too many angels with fiery swords posted at all the gates. The self-concept can only be studied with a great deal of help. This help will consist mainly of two therapeutic aids: one, a study of the barriers erected against perception of the realistic self-concept and, second, the systematic use of feedback procedures to enable the messages to become observable.

DID MARY COVER JONES USE A "PAVLOVIAN" OR AN "INSIGHT" METHOD?

Among the many educational and therapeutic systems of today, it is common to attempt a clean differentiation between the behavior-modification systems and the insight-offering systems. Among the former, there are many methods of objective manipulation of a person's relation to his world. Among the latter may be included those which undertake to define the client's self-image and his attitudes toward this image; the various types of sensitivity training and "encounter" methods also fall into this category. Here there is the confrontation with an external reality or an inner disposition; there is the patient and permissive observation of an unfolding self-realization.

Yet referring back to the methods of outgrowing self-deception, one has to ask whether any confrontation exists that is really *not* at the perceptual-cognitive level, whether the realities encountered are not both "out there" and "in here." It is not difficult to arrange the varieties of undeception systems in chart form, indicating degrees and forms of awareness and unawareness. One may speak with Ralph Hefferline of specific details in a situation in which one becomes aware, or one may speak with Carl Rogers of acceptance of all of one's self. Or one may go in another dimension, a "depth" dimension, "uncovering" layer after layer of dynamically organized material. One might indeed ultimately speak of uncovering (as in the buried city of Troy) all that has grown up from the earliest moment of life. That is, one could accomplish this were it not for the fact that there is a limitless domain, a bottomless pit, a world interminable. Freud remarked that an analysis is over when the patient "ceases to come." By the same token, self-discovery is finished when, from the individual's point of view, "enough" has been found out about the self, when the game has ceased to be worth the candle.

But the quintessence of the "uncovering" approach is "sensitivity training," in which the individual is enabled to come closer and closer to the frightening reality, until his own strength can overpower it (as with Jack and the rabbit). Or in imagination he regards his enemy, his unbearable situation, as a mile away or a year away, or a mile and a year away, and then in imagination brings it to half a mile and a month, or a foot and a minute from where he is. Sensitivity training in this way is the essence or the perfection of direct confrontation. These are devices for making reality more and more acceptable by sheer practice.

To recapitulate, each of the therapeutic methods we have described is to some degree a feedback method. They all help the person to see aspects of himself to which he has been blind. Looking at one's photograph, listening to one's own recorded voice, may be an important beginning. But the messages from *inside* the body have proved to be especially important. For this reason, the research future and the clinical future of further experimental multiple-input studies are likely to be very great indeed. Each person, however, must decide for himself whether the methods of overcoming self-deception as described here can be combined; and if combined, whether they can be integrated into the methods presented in Chapters 5 and 6.

Perhaps most important, each person must decide which method and technique of therapy is most useful and pertinent to himself—to his needs, problems, and approaches to the world, for what works well with one person may not reach another at all. Moreover, a combination of techniques, as with therapeutic drugs, sometimes works far better than a single approach that is more narrowly based. Individualization is critical, since the uniqueness of the person extends to his perceptions and his misperceptions of self, as well.

First of all, the therapist and patient must make up their

minds that the game is worth the effort. Then the therapist has to make a rough appraisal of the patient's current personality, its strengths and weaknesses, as well as they can be perceived initially. Then it is useful to sort out the kinds of techniques and therapy that are most meaningful. For instance, the person who enjoys dramatizing situations might do well in Moreno's psychodrama. The person who enjoys group process might have difficulty with analysis. But let's not be simplistic about this, since occasionally the most unlikely candidate achieves the most with a given technique that is especially alien to his normal modes. A little experimentation is legitimate, but shopping around must not substitute for action in the final analysis. Therapy and change must also fit the pocketbook, time and energy available, and all the other constraints that serve to keep us in a stable rut. Marvelously, however, these somehow are made to fit the need when the determination to change overtakes us.

One must have faith that therapy works, that for each person there are unique ways of breaking out of old routines, fears, prejudices, terrors, hesitations, uncertainties, embarrassments, and inadequacies. One must be willing to try, to find the best and most meaningful techniques that will end in some success. One must look forward to a different, more open self, more comfortable in a wider range of experience, more willing to let the world enter one's life.

CHAPTER 9

―――――

Discipline and Individuality

―――――

WE HAVE at times written as if the individual man or woman could solve the self-deception problem alone. But we are all bound by cultural restraints. Culture can gently mold its human material into a sculptor's gracious forms as Pygmalion molded Galatea, but it can also savagely constrain human nature, chaining it to a Procrustean bed, or it can freeze it into a rigid shape from which there seems to be no escape. The Old Stone Age, permitting mankind surcease from reliance on unshaped club and stone, as nature provided them, slowly allowed our early ancestors to shape their clubs and stones into tools for the hunt, for warfare, and for domestic comforts. As the Old Stone Age passed into the New Stone Age, man, a little more of the artist, fashioned his tools with a little less crudeness.

The discipline of natural necessity yielded slowly to the discipline of newly imagined ways of shaping material. And with the shaping of material came the shaping of folkways, customs, and habits, offering a shared modality of social living, which in time became culture. Constraint, however, in the world of the unfree, could not be loosened for a moment. There were constraints imposed by the material itself and by the physical laws relating to its use. There were constraints imposed by the strong on the weak; by the skilled on the less skilled; and always, of course, the constraints of those adept in the use of symbols on the symbolically inept, who by definition had to accept the code of tribal life. This is to say that there was discipline. Discipline is a rule of life, a mode of ordering human affairs, in which one learns to accept the raw necessity of the things of time and space and the necessity of human interpersonal control. And seeing the world as the group requires, or at times as our society requires, is one of the first principles of discipline, especially of educational and scientific discipline.

One clue to the changing structure of self-understanding lies in new forms of discipline. The development of new forms of discipline marks our modern age, from the mid-nineteenth century to the present. There have, of course, been changes in discipline, slow or rapid, local or general, throughout history, both in the West and in the East. The contrast between preliterate and literate peoples has been partly a matter of the rapidity of changes in codes of life. The world in transition from nomadism to sedentary life, to agriculture, then to commerce and industry, and to science and technology involved constant changes in discipline. For the most part, however, each generation accepted the basic disciplines that their parents had to accept. The tools were usually not changed in just one generation, either in agriculture or in the domestic or business arts or in the arts of science and war. However rapid the changes were, they involved decades or centuries.

What happened, however, in the nineteenth century was quite different. The Napoleonic wars and the British and other colonial systems were set in a context of rapid industrial, then scientific, then technological, then further industrial changes, which (as we read the records and the stories of our own great-grandparents) involved the loss of authority, for the modern scientific comprehension of the universe and the practical application of such knowledge challenged long-held dogmas and authority structures. Consensus and authority faded in the interpretations of religious imperatives and in the ethical and moral codes that had controlled man before the Industrial Revolution and even the more delicate personal world of respect for and deep adherence to parental ways was shaken. All such discipline distinguishes a stable society from an unstable society. By the middle of the nineteenth century, there began a more general rejection of the past, and in our own century there seems to have been a general protest against the rather stable codes that once had represented Western Christian civilization.

Protest is often violent. The opposite of discipline is the rioting Moslems or Hindus in India, the slum dwellers in American cities, who wildly flail about with weapons to hurt or kill. Undisciplined antisocial behavior arouses the anger both of victims and of onlookers. For thousands of years, from the time of the Hammurabi Code, a supposedly "justifiable" reaction to violence has been "an eye for an eye." This punishment had been considered a deterrent to similar actions by others. Yet violent behavior often mounts in response to violence.

Punishment and discipline are thus confused, and when harsh punishment is rationalized as necessary discipline, even for the very young, anger is aroused in them just as it is in any victim. If the young child identifies with the punisher, he continues the pattern toward the next generation, deceiving himself self-righteously, as Samuel Butler described so eloquently in *The Way of All Flesh;* the cruel father considers himself to be the essence of justice.

VARIETIES OF DISCIPLINE

In some liberal circles, recognition of the dangers in harsh punishment and indeed in much arbitrary authoritarian handling of the young (as shown in studies by K. Lewin, R. K.

White, and R. Lippitt) has sometimes led to an equally self-deceiving emphasis on unstructured freedom. But Lewin's group showed that anarchy or a laissez faire approach also leads to destructiveness. They showed that what is needed is considered, thoughtful cooperation between the young and their adult leaders, with motivation for self-discipline developed through agreement growing out of discussion of the consequences of different types of action. Self-discipline turns out to be a form of understanding.

This approach has been developed in a number of schools —even reform schools—as well as in camps and in those homes where adults have learned how to communicate with the young in ways that express their respect for and trust in the child's capacity for control and for cooperation with the group. Along with communication, adults have to provide order, pattern, structure; when the young can live in an organized world from infancy on, they can internalize these structure as a foundation for organizing their lives.

We live today in a discipline-shattered world punctuated by only periodic moments of quiet. Appealing for discipline does not produce it. After a protest riot of any sort, we ask ourselves where all the violence comes from; where all the failures of self-control are driving us; what remains solid as a basis for belief. Youth are caught and whirled aloft in this tempest. It is not merely a question of local and temporal unrest; there is no rest anywhere. The ingredients of Molotov cocktails are to be had for the asking, dynamite obtained with an easy signature, and drugs can be procured from barely hidden pushers in every city and town. The disease is still here. There is often no alternative for youth, accustomed as they are to virtually unlimited expressions of violence on television, exposed to both fictitious and actual wars going on at the moment, with almost no tragedy spared the eyes of the observers, with violence the standard method of cracking down on the violent, and with no codes that are really solidly accepted anywhere among those advancing into maturity. They seek "freedom," but "free" schools can be utterly chaotic or astonishingly creative—depending on the teacher's capacity to help children individually and in the group, to harness their drives, and to channel vital energies into productive activity.

Technological and social change put the codes and assumptions of parents in the position of being irrelevant to the new conditions of life experienced by children and youth. The younger generation has increasingly protested the euphemisms, masks, polite deceits, and hidden brutalities of adult life and has begun to strike out for honesty. Many of the children of adults who had devoted their lives to "trying to make the world better" have renounced the pattern of their parents' pressured mode of living and opted for discovering a different and better life for themselves, including a variety of styles free from rigid structures and authoritarian discipline.

Other lines of change in the direction of individual fulfillment and group cooperation are evoked by reactions against the materialism and the stereotyping of life contributed by the forces of industry (as illustrated by Whyte's "organization man"). The business and political establishments flourish with their own coercive codes and their adulation of the successful, the financial elite paying little attention to the freedom buffs.

It may be maintained that the discipline of scientific method remains intact among the decaying externally imposed disciplines, which can no longer command the unchallenged loyalty of modern people. Indeed, science is rapidly gaining a peremptory command over thoughtful minds. Science determines *how* things must be done and undone, and there is no escape.

Thus, for example, biochemistry and physiology yield nerve gases, which later need to be buried under the sea. But science in its present shape does not determine *where* or *when* the nerve gases and all their likes are to be used or submerged. Here military, political, and ethical demands whirl in unresolved conflict, and the decision has to be made without adequate analysis or knowledge of consequences. There is no scientific discipline yet available to guide us through critical decisions. Science offers a clear discipline only when its content, its method, and its relevance are clear.

There can indeed ultimately be a more comprehensive science, a deeply probing science of man, which can have this disciplinary power over our decisions, and it is this kind of science—one that turns inward to a study of the nature of man as well as outwardly upon the reciprocities between men—that the present analysis attempts to support. The sciences dealing with human nature will have to achieve an authority equal to that of physics; they will have to show what kind of a "human nature" can survive; they will have to show more fully and more clearly *the nature of man's self-deception and the levels of outgrowing it.*

THE DISCIPLINE OF RELATIVITY

The whole movement away from the firm and absolute codes of life—the religion, morals, and "common sense" by which a few hundred years ago one had to live—have yielded to a general readiness to approach every problem as if it could be decided by its context, if not by an immediate context, then by a more remote one, and if not by a more remote one, then by the whole of reality. There are thus no right and wrong procedures, only better and worse ones. Relativity theory in physics and astronomy becomes a guide to relativism in matters of art, law, and ethics. This is a kind of code, a kind of first principle, a kind of discipline: "Never stop to decide a question until the judgments of the stars in their courses have been made." Ancient fatalism, Eastern and Western, and perhaps modern astrologies as well, have won their popularity through appeal to this conviction that each human act has its cosmic context. Of course, this implies also that we need to know everything before we can decide anything. This is about the same as saying that we have no code to live by, since we cannot know very much about these larger cosmic contexts. The upshot of this whole way of thinking is to lead many to decide that relativity really offers no discipline at all. It is what we know of man's evolutionary nature and latent potentialities, and what we can learn tomorrow, that will be critical. And this kind of knowledge will be available only when unwitting self-deception is on the way out.

In the meantime, people who try to get rid of self-deceptions can be very great nuisances indeed. Henrik Ibsen understood this well. A physician who rejoiced in the curative powers of local mineral waters suddenly had to face up to the fact that the waters were useless and in fact dangerous, and he became "The Enemy of the People." The abolitionists observed that the slave trade was damaging not only to the souls of the blacks but to those of the whites, and were regarded as "extremists." It took the emotional blast of *Uncle Tom's Cabin*, the Civil War, and a century of struggle to get a factual focus on the question of the actual consequences of economic exploitation upon personal and national character.

"Let us keep our self-deception," say my friends. The greatest of the great have their blessed self-deception. The battle between Leibniz and Newton is altogether incredible to those who know them only as great mathematicians. They tore at each other like tigers; they were the Lord's anointed, and each knew it. We need scarcely take the space to describe the intensity of their belief in themselves and in their rightness. And who can say that this kind of overweening self-image is damaging, either to individuals or to humankind? Can we honestly say that Beethoven, who saw himself as a direct channel for God's message, was in any sense "mistaken"

[123]

—what do we know of such ultimate messages, we who are not Beethovens? And who can say that the "cosmic" religion of Einstein is a delusion simply because it has not the same objective demonstrability as the relativity tests, such as the bending of light around an object or the strange behavior of the invisible "companion of Sirius"?

What a nuisance, however, is any proposal aimed at reducing the accepted, comfortable level of self-deception! Our goal must be to show the inherent humanness and at times both the promise and the dangers inherent in it. Just as Beethoven made majestic and overwhelming discoveries in the only partially explored regions of tone and rhythm, and just as Freud, battling the physicians of Vienna, pulled down upon himself the condemnation of medical and scientific respectability, so a certain very large dose of overbelief in oneself seems to be necessary to the world of great discovery.

This inflation of self, however, though very common among geniuses, does not seem to be inherent in all genius as such. Charles Darwin, quietly and firmly aware of the magnitude of his discovery, remained humbly, realistically, simply, a man of science. Einstein, bold in his science, bold even in his philosophy, remained simple, casual, approachable, an undemonstrative discoverer who after his tremendous contributions tried steadily to go further, recognizing that his capacities had their limits and that his own contribution was just one corner of a growing cosmology.

Perhaps the value of self-deception in some cases—and the value of outgrowing self-deception in other cases—depends on the sheer magnitude and relevance of what is discovered through each of these contrasting methods. John Berdan, who taught English literature at Yale over half a century ago, was asked how important it really was to write simply and clearly. "Well," he said, "the greatest book of the nineteenth century is the *Origin of Species* and it's not particularly well written. The answer is that if you are Niagara Falls, you will crash down and nothing will stop you. But if you are a garden hose, you'd better eliminate the kinks when you water your lawn." Some kinds of self-deception are kinks in the garden hose.

Other forms of self-deception, however, block not only an individual scientist but a whole era from grasping the patent reality to which new investigations are pointing. As T. S. Kuhn points out in *The Structure of Scientific Revolutions*, a new era in science does not present itself when the factual basis for a new scientific approach is offered. A new theory must be pinpointed that will explain both the old facts and the new facts. Perhaps he should have added that a scientific revolution can occur only when the personal investment in the safe, strong, reputable, grand old system is no longer safer or more reputable than a new system buttressed by both clear facts and by clear theory. If the image of the self, as pioneer facing the new, becomes worthy of respect, the old can shrivel away.

THE DISCIPLINE
OF INDIVIDUALITY

The truth has been dawning upon us in this century that the Victorian fear of the body prevented various types of self-realization that had been very precious to the Greek world, and to the Renaissance, which mediated the Greek world to us moderns. Specifically, it was the anatomical knowledge of the body, as seen, for example, in sculpture, in a medical atlas, or in Sheldon's body photographs, that taught us to see the interrelations of various self-revealing functions which we have briefly and inadequately touched upon here.

In Figure 5 one notes the word *individuality* in capital letters, at the center, as a guide to the amazing array of forms

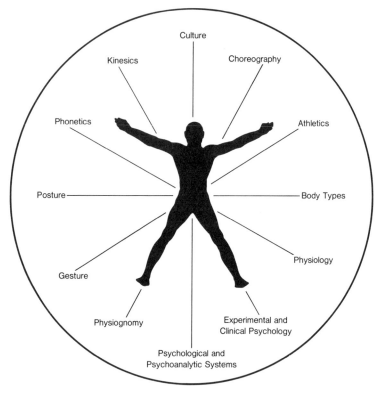

Figure 5. Human Individuality.

of human investigation centered in the body that are important for self-realization and for the overcoming of self-deception. Above and to the right of the word *individuality* stands the word *choreography*, to indicate the role of the dance in the fulfillment of the body, in the position to which we would assign a "1" on the face of a clock. At 2 o'clock stands *athletics* (and athletic coaching, as for the Olympic games). At 3 o'clock the physician's or the anthropologist's three-dimensional study of *body types*; at 4, *physiology*, including, of course, *neurophysiology*; at 5, *experimental and clinical psychology*; and at 6, the *psychological and psychoanalytic systems* that deal with the whole person as a psychophysical unit. At 7 o'clock appears *physiognomy*, the study of faces; and at 8, the study of *hands* and *gesture*, the expressive totality of the body. We allow space for *posture* at 9; this moves us to the world of the stage, including the actor's use of gesture, posture, and voice. We find ourselves led on at 10 o'clock to *phonetics*, especially the expressive value of speech utterances; and with it the world of *kinesics* at 11, with which much of this graph is indirectly concerned, since kinesics is an expression of functional anatomy; that is, of physiology, as well as of the more culturally stylized expressive function. At 12 stands *culture*, in which the meanings, especially the symbolic meanings of the person in action in a group setting, are investigated, with special emphasis upon language and upon those aspects of material culture that are most intimately related to the human body and its work, such as the various pure and applied arts, including music and poetry. The interaction of these functions is *individualized* into a unique pattern in which each of these expressive aspects of a life can be seen in a form which occurs once and never is seen again.

INDIVIDUAL DIFFERENCES

To do justice to the rich individual differences in the pattern of self-deceptive strategies by which we live would require a systematic survey of the whole field of modern "cognitive psychology" and its special studies of "cognitive style." Some people are constantly looking for differences, and finding them, others looking for similarities and finding them. Some people establish a direction and swing along gaily in one associative track; others start and stop and move more with a *staccato* than with a *glissando* type of expression. In the extensive studies of H. A. Witkin and his associates, people are graded on a scale from extreme *field dependence* (allowing even dominant elements in the perceptual field to be muted or distorted by the background) as contrasted with *field independence*, in which the central presentation is sharply separated off, as by a cookie-cutter, from the background material. In the Menninger Foundation studies by Riley Gardner and his associates, a strong case is made for the presence of several large personality dispositions or factors, each reliably measurable, which enable each perceiver to perceive, remember, and conceptualize in his own way.

These important issues are not discussed here, since our task is simply to note the general dynamics of self-deception and modes of overcoming it. It is necessary, however, to emphasize the fact that every act of perceiving, remembering, and thinking expresses some individuality derived from personal cognitive style; and since each cognitive act is selective, the appreciation and the inclusion of one aspect of the situation involves the exclusion or muting of other aspects of the situation.

Each of us can rightly say that his or her style of self-deception is unique. What we gain in reality at one point, we are likely to lose at another—that is, in adroit gamesmanship in battling ourselves. While not wishing to commit ourselves to the Freudian notion of a limited fund of energy that has to be hoarded and spent in accordance with a strict economic principle, we do agree that the process of exclusion of *some* information is almost by definition a matter of accentuation of *other* information. In a figure-ground situation, for example, we see one pattern and thereby relegate another to a secondary position. In pursuing somewhat guiltily a fascinating taboo theme, we give it major attention and remain only vaguely aware of the accompanying guilt. Self-deception is always a matter of relative accentuation of one, as opposed to another, way of confronting reality.

It may be that curiosity is an exception and that there really are conflict-free ego spheres, in which there is no conflict between materials present in our awareness. The issue is not altogether resolved. Regardless of curiosity theory and the conception of pure cognitive function, there always appears to be a competition among the ways in which cognitive life may be expressed, and we *always* seem to pay a considerable price when we attend to anything, because in the too-much-ness of life, we cannot take in everything at once. Even simplification is only a partial solution, for there is always the danger of stimulus deprivation, wherein if you eliminate the outer pressures, the inner pressures become unbearable. Much work is needed before we can learn to gain protection against excessive bombardment from without and from within.

DEVELOPING STRAIGHT THINKING

The capacity to develop generalized habits of confronting reality has long been the subject of educational research. Partly under John Dewey's influence on the idea of education in straight thinking, and partly as a result of increased understanding of the role of propaganda in distorting political thought, studies of opinion-change became widespread; the aim has been to see whether a generalized capacity for straight thinking could actually be built into the individual. A pioneer study of exceptional skill was made by Goodwin Watson in 1925. He devised a test of "fair-mindedness," as contrasted with biased thinking, relating to a wide variety of issues and a wide variety of ways of measuring the bias which appeared in relation to each kind of issue: political, economic, racial, religious, social class, and so on. There were so many elements chosen that he could legitimately comb through each individual's responses to the whole test and show the general disposition (not just the bias in respect to single issues) that resulted in high or low prejudice scores. As a matter of fact, the test of internal consistency came off very well. It turned out that there really were people with *generalized* straight thinking and people with *generalized* susceptibility to bias, with most subjects, of course, ranging in between.

Later on, Rensis Likert and I studied another type of generalized prejudice by means of the social-distance test devised by Emory Bogardus. The internal consistency of the test is so great that if you know the total amount of prejudice against a random *half* of the nations mentioned, such as Armenians, Belgians, Canadians, Danes, Finns, Greeks, Hungarians, Italians, Japanese, you can predict *almost exactly* the total prejudice that will be shown against the other half, such as Nigerians, Pakistanis, Poles, Rumanians, Swedes, Turks, Ukrainians, Venezuelans. Eugene Hartley confirmed this with a fresh and very large number of students at different institutions and again found the attitudes toward foreign groups to be very highly generalized. He went on to make up a list of imaginary national groups such as Danireans, Pierians, and Wallonians; toward all of these nonexistent groups the degree of social distance was just about the same as toward the real groups. There are, of course, plenty of biases that are *not* generalized, but there *is* such a thing as generalized bias, and such a thing as generalized freedom from bias.

Now the critical questions arise. Can generalized freedom from bias be trained? Can it be built in? This has been the subject of abundant research, particularly by E. M. Glaser. Before asking a group of students to analyze newspaper material that contained much propaganda, some were taught something about the psychology of thinking and were given practice in the recognition of errors. After four weeks, the four groups of experimental classes were significantly more fair-minded than the control classes that had had no such training.

But the issue is more complicated. We saw that Biddle trained his students to detect propaganda in reports (p. 108) on the Atlantic and Caribbean relations characteristic of American foreign policy. Then, after the passage of some weeks, he presented them with similar reports on the Pacific relations of the United States. We would assume that in American newspapers and other public material there would be some resemblance between kinds of bias entering into reporting on the Atlantic and Caribbean issues and in reporting on the Pacific issues; and in fact it turned out in practice that students who had been trained to understand the former could make a transfer to the new material dealing with the Pacific, although not a single stated issue was the same. The students, in other words, showed some result of their training in being able to check up on newspaper biases and their own biases. Most significant, the students who really understood the *nature* of biased reporting and thinking, who saw into the character of the communication problem, were the ones most able to make the transfer.

Perhaps there is a lesson to be learned in all of this regarding straight thinking. Social-scientific method offers only a beginning for us, with careful, systematic analysis of evidence and a few suggestions on how best to get started. The difficulty here is to apply this technique to that most slippery of substances: our own attitudes and approaches to our most precious, closely held beliefs. Lin Yutang describes this initial stumblingblock delightfully in the preface to his *From Pagan to Christian:* "But though many private persons think almost as highly of their own infallibility as that of their sect, few express it so naturally as a certain French lady, who, in a little dispute with her sister, said, 'But I meet with nobody but myself that is always in the right,' '*Je ne trouve que moi qui aie toujours raison.*' "

In Chapter 10 we will discuss how some have overcome this stumbling block.

CHAPTER 10

External Forces and
Internal Change

THEORY has been useful so far, but now it may be more valuable to examine how some individuals have actually conducted their search for a personal grail of honest perception and objectivity. We will first peruse the testimony of some persons who have experienced trauma that helped to set them on the "straight" path. In Chapter 11 we will then study some of those who have deliberately devoted their lives to the search for truth in the face of inertia or social opposition and have left a rich heritage of shared experience.

When a great personal change is being readied, there is a preparation within the mind. It is as if the stones on the road to change were being removed, the soil being raked and smoothed, in anticipation of the top layer of asphalt to be laid. While the change that occurs may appear to be rapid, in actuality there has been much preparation beforehand setting the mental stage for the change.

Several individuals in recent history can be used as examples of this apparently rapid shift in views and values, individuals who experienced a sudden sensation that the scales had been lifted from their eyes, and that they saw the world clearly for the first time.

Conversely, when the return to a former point of view is being readied, the old questions emerge from the once-dominant sector of the mind and an older personality and outlook prepares, like a government-in-exile, to take over once again.

INSTANT REAPPRAISAL

Clifford W. Beers had been hospitalized for more than two years, all that time in the depressive phase of a manic-depressive psychosis—mute and subject to severe delusions about the nature of the real world. He prepared for suicide by drowning, but at the same time worked out an elaborate stratagem to communicate with his brother, George. He believed that imposters were visiting him, but that his real family still lived at their old address. Through a fellow patient he sent a letter to George, requesting a visit. The emotional investment in this effort was considerable—it was the first letter he had written in twenty-six months. The dramatic result follows, in Beers's own words from *A Mind that Found Itself*:

The person approaching me was indeed the counterpart of my brother as I remembered him. Yet he was no more my brother than he had been at any time during the preceding two years. He was still a detective. Such he was when I shook his hand. As soon as that ceremony was over, he drew forth a leather pocketbook. I instantly recognized it as one I myself had carried for several years prior to the time I was taken ill in 1900. It was from this that he took my recent letter.

"Here's my passport," he said.

"It's a good thing you brought it," I replied, as I glanced at it and again shook his hand—this time the hand of my own brother.

"Don't you want to read it?" he asked.

"There is no need of that. I am convinced."

After my long journey of exploration in the jungle of a tangled imagination, a journey which finally ended in my finding the person for whom I had long searched, my behavior differed very little from that of a great explorer who, full of doubt after a long and perilous trip through real jungles, found the man he sought and, grasping his hand, greeted him with the simple and historic words, "Dr. Livingstone, I presume?"

The very instant I caught sight of my letter in the hands of my brother, all was changed. The thousands of false impressions recorded during the seven hundred and ninety-eight days of my depression seemed at once to correct themselves. Untruth became Truth. A large part of what was once my old world was again mine. To me, at least, my mind seemed to have found itself, for the gigantic web of false beliefs in which it had been all but hopelessly enmeshed I now immediately recognized as a snare of delusions. That the Gordian knot of mental torture should be cut and swept away by the mere glance of a willing eye is like a miracle. Not a few patients, however, suffering from certain forms of mental disorder, regain a high degree of insight into their mental condition in what might be termed a flash of divine enlightenment. Though insight regained seemingly in an instant is a most encouraging symptom, power to reason normally on all subjects cannot, of course, be so promptly recovered. My new power to reason correctly on some subjects simply marked the transition from depression, one phase of my disorder, to elation, another phase of it. Medically speaking, I was as mentally disordered as before—yet I was happy!

My memory during depression may be likened to a photographic film, seven hundred and ninety-eight days long. Each impression seems to have been made in a negative way and then, in a fraction of a second, miraculously developed and made positive. Of hundreds of impressions made during that depressed period I had not before been conscious, but from the moment my mind, if not my full reason, found itself, they stood out vividly. Not only so, but other impressions registered during earlier years became clearer. Since that August 30th, which I regard as my second birthday (my first was on the 30th of another month), my mind has exhibited qualities which, prior to that time, were so latent as to be scarcely distinguishable. As a result, I find myself able to do desirable things I never before dreamed of doing—the writing of this book is one of them.

Beers, of course, used these charged energies of the manic phase to go on to a distinguished career in the development of the mental hygiene movement in the United States. The turning of the hinge of his personal fate seemed instantaneous, but in actuality it had been prepared in the months preceding the event by a series of psychic shifts that set the stage for his reintegration of the world into a self more socially satisfying and acceptable to others.

THE PERCEPTION OF WE AND THEY

Stephen Spender, the English poet, came to a significant conclusion about the self-perceptions of "we and they," in the highly charged political world of the Spanish Civil War. In an essay in *The God that Failed* he notes:

At this time, I came to a conclusion which, although it may appear obvious, was important to development of my thinking about politics. This was simply that nearly all human beings have an extremely intermittent grasp on reality. Only a few things, which illustrate their own interests and ideas, are real to them. Other things, which are in fact equally real, appear to them as abstractions. Thus, when men have decided to pursue a course of action, everything which serves to support this seems vivid and real; everything which stands against it becomes abstraction. Your friends are allies and therefore real human beings with flesh and blood and sympathies like yourself. Your opponents are just tiresome, unreasonable, unnecessary theses, whose lives are so many false statements which you would like to strike out with a lead bullet as you would put the stroke of lead pencil through a bungled paragraph.

Not to think this way demands the most exceptional qualities of judicious-mindedness or of high imaginative understanding. During the Spanish War it dismayed me to notice that I thought like this myself. When I saw photographs of children murdered by the Fascists, I felt furious pity. When the supporters of Franco talked of Red atrocities, I merely felt indignant that people should tell such lies. In the first case I saw corpses, in the second only words. However, I never learned to be unself-critical, and thus I gradually acquired a certain horror of the way in which my own mind worked. It was clear to me that unless I cared about every murdered child impartially, I did not really care about children being murdered at all. I was performing an obscene mental act on certain corpses which became the fuel for propagandist passions, but I showed my fundamental indifference by not caring about those other corpses who were the victims of the Republicans.

SELF-PERCEPTION OF DIFFERENCE

Will Thomas, in his book *The Seeking,* portrays the staggering moment when a young child becomes aware of his difference from the majority society. It is a universal experience for all minorities, stigmatized persons, and those who have a significant cultural difference that they carry for much or most of their lives.

"Looka here, Willie," Jess said quietly, "how come you don't like to be called 'nigger'? You don't think you are a Peck, do you? . . ."

"Well," I said, fumbling to explain what I did not understand, "it is a bad word. You fight a guy that calls it to you."

"You fight a *white* guy that calls you that," Jess corrected. "You fight a Peck when he calls you that or 'darky' or 'coon' or 'Sambo' or 'snowball.' "

A dim light was dawning, a foggy understanding. I said, "Those guys we were fighting—they were all white? Is that why you call them Pecks?"

"Well, gah-ah-ah-dam!" Mike exclaimed unbelievingly. "You tryna say you don't know what a Peck is—a Peckerwood? Where you been all your life, man?"

"Why—why in Chicago," I said bewilderedly.

Jess laughed. "Hey, Willie, didn't you sure 'nough know what a Peck was?"

"I thought it was the name of a gang," I confessed, ashamed of what now seemed a colossal ignorance, "like in Chicago. We called our gang the 'Dearborn Street Sluggers,' because we lived on Dearborn Street. But mostly we just called ourselves 'The Dearborns.' So when you said we were going to fight the Pecks, I just thought—"

Jess laughed. Mike whistled as though amazed. Jess dropped an arm around my shoulders and said, "Willie, you got a lot to learn." I tried to hold back the tears, but they came and I began to blubber

[136]

and Mike gave me a punch in the back, not hard, and said, "Well, it ain't nothing to cry about, Willie."

It was a good moment, but also one of confusion about many matters still unclear. I gulped and scrubbed away my tears and Jess and Mike sat down on the curbing, with me between them, and Jess put his arm around me again and gave me a squeeze and said gruffly, "Everything's all right, Willie," and Mike said wonderingly, "So *that's* how come you popped Jake that day in the park! I'll be doggoned. You *sure* got a lot to learn, boy. . . ."

Mike thawed completely during that strange session when I was initiated into the society to which I had not known I belonged, for I had not known it even existed.

When that day began, I was but a boy. At its end I had become a *Negro* boy, and as such, for the first time, troubledly glimpsed walls which, like morning mists, arose between people different in something called race.

IN AND OUT OF RELIGIOUS BELIEF

Tolstoy experienced several conversions and reconversions during his lifetime, always making the pilgrimage first within his own soul—the social metamorphosis came later. At the point where he was about to plunge into orthodox Christianity he wrote: "As soon as man applies his intelligence and only his intelligence to any object at all, he unfailingly destroys the object." Troyat, in his book *Tolstoy*, then writes:

One spring day when he was walking in the forest, his mind suddenly felt lighter and his whole body began to move more freely through the light-spattered dimness. Intrigued, he observed that he was always sad when he rejected God with his reason and always cheerful when he accepted him like a child.

"At the thought of God, happy waves of life welled up inside me," he wrote. "Everything came alive, took on meaning. The moment I thought I knew God, I lived. But the moment I forgot him, the moment I stopped believing, I also stopped living. . . . To know God and to live are the same thing. God is life."

He had found faith. A faith within reach of all. Like a shipwrecked man at the end of his strength, Tolstoy clung to this raft.

First, he saw that he could only remain in his state of grace by accepting it unconditionally. Even if certain rituals of the faithful seemed silly and unjustifiable to him, even if the behavior of the faithful resembled blind superstition, he must obey the law of the flock or be lost. God, as creator of the entire world, could only have revealed his truth to all men, united by love. To pray to God by oneself was an absurdity. It was necessary to pray to him among the masses, through the masses. With the same energy he had formerly applied to reviling the dogma of the Orthodox Church, Tolstoy now threw himself into piety. He who had even refused to attend the services in the house organized by Sonya for feast days now began to say his prayers morning and night without any prompting from anyone; he got up early for mass on Sunday, confessed and took communion, fasted on Wednesdays and Fridays.

"I know that what I am doing is right," he said, "if only because, in order to mortify the pride of spirit, be united with my ancestors and fellow men and continue my search for the meaning of life, I am sacrificing my physical comfort."

For nearly two years, he accepted the Church conformingly.

On May 22, 1878 he wrote in his diary, "Went to mass Sunday. I can find a satisfactory explanation for everything that happens during the service. But wishing 'long life' (to the tsar) and praying for victory over our enemies are sacrilege. A Christian should pray for his enemies, not against them." This was the beginning of schism.

Other parts of the service gradually began to come into conflict with his common sense, and even with the teachings of Christ. After refusing to let himself question a single word of the dogma, he now began to pick it to pieces, word by word, not as a skeptic but in the manner of one of the early Christians, still illuminated by the *historical* proximity of the Lord. He admired the ethical laws preached by the apostles, but he did not believe in the resurrection of Christ because he could not imagine it actually happening. He also balked at the celebration of the miracles—Ascension, Pentecost, the Annunciation, the Intercession of the Blessed Virgin. To his mind all that was a product of cheap imagery, unworthy of the cause of God. "To reinforce the teachings of Christ with miracles," he wrote in his notebook, "is like holding a lighted candle in front of the sun in order to see it better."

Still more absurd and pointless, in his opinion, were the mysteries, especially baptism and Eucharist. And besides, why did the Orthodox Church, whose mission should be to bring about an alliance between all men, treat the Roman Catholics and Protestants—who worshipped the same God—as heretics? Why, in the same breath as it commanded the faithful to be charitable and forgive those who trespassed against them, did it pray for the champion of the poor and disinherited, swathed in gold and precious stones and damasks? . . .

One morning . . . as he was preparing to take communion, the priest called upon him to affirm that the body and blood of Jesus Christ were literally present in the consecrated bread and wine. He was suddenly disturbed and annoyed by this ritual question he had heard hundreds of times before; he felt something like a knife-thrust near his heart, and stammered out a faltering "yes;" but he knew as he came out of the little country church that he would never touch the bread of life again. One Wednesday—a fast-day—when the whole family was sitting down together for the evening meal, he pushed away the porridge and pointing to a dish of meatballs that had been prepared for the two non-fasting tutors, frowned at his son Ilya and growled aggressively, "Pass the meat!" No one dared express surprise. Before the entire mute but smirking table, the master of Yasnaya Polyana defiantly began to chew the forbidden food.

Lin Yutang, in the preface to his book *From Pagan to Christian*, observes:

This is therefore necessarily a story of personal experience, for all worth-while accounts of this kind must necessarily be based on personal inquiry, on moments of doubt and moments of insight and intimation. . . . It is by no means a smooth voyage of discovery, but one full of spiritual shocks and encounters. There is always something of the story of Jacob's wrestling with God in his dream; for the search for truth is seldom a pleasure cruise. There were storms and shipwrecks and puzzling deviations of the magnetic compass which frightened the sailors on Christopher Columbus' boat. There were doubts, hesitancies and threats of mutiny, and the desire to turn back. I had to sail past the Scylla of a damning hellfire and the Charybdis of Pharisaism, Scribism, and Caiaphatism of organized belief. I finally got through. But it has been worth while.

CHAPTER 11

The (Usually) Undeceived: The Lifetime Search

WE HAVE LEARNED a little here and there about man's fabulous capacity to look and not see, to listen and not hear, or, indeed, to give up both looking and listening. One might be tempted to close on a note of pessimism. This would, however, miss the point. In the preceding chapter, we saw a few personal incidents in the reality quest. Better still, there are genuine discoveries that can be shared with others, and that can become part of our heritage. Here and there individuals in history have grasped reality in a firm clutch and have carried it through confusion and ridicule to establish new beachheads on the way to realities significant for human living. Here and there, something can be learned from the study of such lives—lives devoted to truth with either a large T or a small one, depending on our mood, our own preferred balance between pride in human achievements and a humility engendered by their pitiful limitations. We can learn something by looking at the work of such individuals —those successful battlers against self-deceptions, all exceptional samples of a kind of rare humanity who have looked for truth in a joyful and lightsome spirit or, if need be, with a fierce and steady gaze. We may ask who among us has developed the most effective methods of unblinding himself, who has been especially astute or courageous, or both, in contriving effective ways of freeing himself from personal self-deceptions or from the self-deceptions of his group? In this last chapter, our focus is not on the general problem of pursuit of social and personal truth in the abstract, but on a specific, historical-psychological study of concrete individual efforts, successfully directed to specific goals over a lifetime. This will involve looking at the history of science and of the arts, philosophies, and patterns of social living that, in exceptional eyes and hands, yielded exceptionally rich knowledge about how self-deception can be overcome.

The emancipation of the individual from self-deception depends on two principles: (1) a system of practical personal guidelines toward clear confrontation of reality; (2) the development of a clear picture of self as a reality seeker. The lure toward self-image distortion can find its match in the determination to encounter the delights of *real* reality.

The individuals chosen are historically significant innovators. Of course, to cultivate a new self-image is each individual's privilege—from an individualistic point of view. From the social point of view, however, there is always more to be said than what the individual *can* say about the self he thinks he is discovering. Each individual self is found in a matrix of almost infinite richness and subtlety, with roles, tasks, and identification changing hourly and with each role a form of "presentation of self" in which other forms of presentation always remain possible and which will, in fact, take their turn in appearing. A volume written from an individualistic point of view can aim at an ever-widening vista of possibilities for self-discovery until the individual calls a halt. But others looking down from a second-story window into the street of social interaction will always see more.

[141]

In these last pages, we shall try to portray some individual forms of struggle toward reality, as seen in the West from the viewpoints that we call Socratic, Stoic, Epicurean, Augustinian, Copernican, Franklinian, Darwinian, Freudian, Einsteinian. We shall also offer a brief word about the Asian systems as well. These forms of personal redemption from private folly into human or cosmic reality-contact represent more than the wish for reality and the craving to believe that it is to be had by man; they seem to represent genuine truth-seeking devices, discoverable by individuals and communicable from one to another; they do, in fact, broaden the circle of awareness of reality, both external and internal.

SOCRATES

If you ask yourself why Socrates was not afraid to die, you may reach the conviction that the quest of ultimate realities may yield immediate pragmatic results, may in fact give continuous practical meaning to everyday decisions. He was publicly tried by the men of Athens for "not worshipping the gods whom the city worshipped," and for "corrupting the youth." He pointed out that his legs might easily have carried him off to some point of safety, but that reality seemed to make it better to die as he had lived, facing issues rather than escaping them. As Socrates prepared to drink the hemlock, he continued to discuss quietly with his friends the question of the nature of truth and of the good. Socrates' philosophy may have been technically in error, but it was a philosophy that made possible a genuine adaptation to reality or indeed a discovery of the human realities that all Western philosophy has embraced. His guiding principle was: Truth is worth more than life.

STOICS AND EPICUREANS

In the centuries after the life of Socrates, there developed two great systems of Greek and Roman philosophy, the Stoic and the Epicurean. The Stoic was based firmly upon the principle of living "according to nature." All the effort of study and discipline was devoted to the conception of the natural. It was a matter of order, natural order, and a human order in concord with it. The Roman Emperor Marcus Aurelius exemplifies the simple Stoic discipline of cultivation of truth, which the higher levels of Roman civilization expressed. In his *Meditations* (translated by M. H. Morgan) he notes:

From Apollonius I learned freedom of will and undeviating steadiness of purpose; and to look to nothing else, not even for a moment, except to reason; and to be always the same, in sharp pains, on the occasion of the loss of a child, and in long illness; and to see clearly in a living example that the same man can be both most resolute and yielding, and not peevish in giving his instruction; and to have had before my eyes a man who clearly considered his experience and his merits; and from him I learned how to receive from friends what are esteemed favors, without being either humbled by them or letting them pass unnoticed. . . .

From Catullus, not to be indifferent when a friend finds fault, even if he should do so without reason, but to try to restore him to his usual disposition; and to be ready to speak well of teachers, as it is reported of Domitius and Athenodotus; and to love my children truly.

From my brother, Severus, to love my kin, and to love truth, and to love justice; and through him I learned to know Thrasea, Helvidius, Cato, Dion, Brutus; and from him I received the idea of a polity in which there is the same law for all, a polity administered with regard to equal rights and equal freedom of speech, and the idea of a kingly government which respects most of all the freedom of the governed; I learned from him also: consistency and undeviating steadiness in my regard for philosophy, and a disposition to do good, and to give to others readily, and to cherish good hopes, and to believe that I am loved by my friends; and in him I observed no concealment of his opinions with respect to those whom he condemned, and that his friends had no need to conjecture what he wished or did not wish, but it was quite plain.

From Maximus I learned self-government, and not to be led aside by anything; and cheerfulness in all circumstances, as well as in illness; and a just admixture in the moral character of sweetness and dignity, and to do what was set before me without complaining. I observed that everybody believed that he thought as he spoke, and that in all that he did he never had any bad intention. . . .

In my father I observed mildness of temper, and unchangeable resolution in the things which he had determined after due deliberation; and no vainglory in those things which men call honors; and a love of labor and perseverance; and a readiness to listen to those who had anything to propose for the commonweal; and undeviating firmness in giving to every man according to his deserts.

From our modern Western viewpoint, the contrast between Stoicism and Epicureanism appears to overemphasize their differences, outweighing their fundamental uniformities. Epicurus, viewing the universality of human suffering, admonished his students to avoid the distress caused by momentary or superficial pleasures; he urged that if true and enduring happiness is to be cultivated, it must involve a life of order, rationality, and restraint. Often it was publicly assumed that the Epicureans were men given to high living, but in fact it was only high in the sense that it was rationally and humanely ordered. Epicurus believed firmly, moreover, in the capacity of the philosopher to share democratically with men of all walks of life, and with women, too, in the great school that he founded—a rather extraordinary exhibition of trust in the liberated mind wherever it is found.

In these philosophies, there is no clear conception of transgression; the disharmony of man and man led in time to a conception of temptation and sin. The conception of sin developed in Zoroastrianism (in which the dark forces of Ahriman opposed the light of Ahura-mazda), and led to more and more searching for the basis of ways in which men had strayed from the right path, craving the salvation that called for a redeeming force. This force was stressed by the Greek "mystery religions," by Judaism, and by the Christian Church fathers, notably by Saint Paul. He expressed the democratic struggle of the early Church to include every man, woman, and child, from emperor to slave, from Jew to Greek to Ethiopian, partly through the development of a conception of destiny in which all mankind was eligible for a redeeming rebirth. This redemption, however, could not be solely a matter of intellect. The perspective on larger human issues could be given only when the human soul accepted the redemptive role of a divine savior. The development of these thoughts led to the first great book of inner confrontation, the autobiography of Saint Augustine, *The Confessions*. One learns to face oneself, to see in detachment the strengths and weaknesses, and above all, the areas of contradiction and possible reconciliation within the inner world. Saint Augustine represents a discipline of self-confrontation.

COPERNICUS AND GALILEO

As one turns over the great pages to the age of *science*—to Copernicus and Galileo in the heyday of the Renaissance— one finds the same principle of discipline holding fast. Copernicus, however, understood more precisely the discipline of objective evidence and how to subject it to rational analysis. Modern studies of Copernicus have shown that his method was very far indeed from the quick and easy perception of a necessary reality. On the contrary, as a boy and young man he was steeped in astronomical studies. He spent several decades subjecting each new theoretical advance to logical analysis. Greek models of a heliocentric universe were at hand, and the evidence in favor of such a scheme acted slowly and inexorably upon him like the acid of the engraver. Since he had subjected earlier formulations, including his own, to refinement, he could finally offer a heliocentric system that had the discipline of refined observations to support it.

Even so, however, he did not altogether succeed in pruning away his self-deceptions. It had been assumed in the great tradition of astronomy that nature's data must be "perfect"; that is, they must obey a mathematical order of beauty or excellence. So far, so good. But in the Greek tradition it had been assumed that the circle is "perfect" in two dimensions and the sphere "perfect" in three dimensions, so that heavenly bodies must of course move in circular paths, and that each of them must be a sphere. The actual astronomical data of Copernicus's time were not really reconcilable with these notions, and it began to be clear, in the further data coming to hand after the time of Copernicus, that the paths of the planets about the sun are *not* circles, but ellipses. This self-deception (that nature is "perfect" in the sense of conforming to human ideals) was a cultural deception; the self-deception involved in seeking this kind of "perfection" had to yield to the fresh empirical realities offered by fresh astronomical observation.

Galileo was also looking for perfect, Platonic-mathematical exemplifications of nature's perfect laws. With Galileo, however, the supremacy of empirical work—actually watching falling bodies—forced experimental physics into the center of the new knowledge as it forced the sun into the center of the solar system. Then, a British physician, William Harvey, maintaining that the heart works "like a water pump," visited Galileo in 1608 and was electrified by the new experimental mechanics of the master whom he saw at Padua. Harvey's published work on the circulation of the blood marked a tremendous advance in the empirical studies of the body. The naturalism of the new science could be applied to all things, both nonliving and living.

FRANKLIN

This naturalism could be applied to man himself. When we recall Benjamin Franklin's bringing the lightning into his Leyden jar, we may think of his attempt to rebuild himself by remedying his habits, especially his habits of self-deception. In his *Autobiography* he describes his analytical, experimental method of self-correction:

I made a little book, in which I allotted a page for each of the virtues. I rul'd each page with red ink, so as to have seven columns, one for each day of the week, marking each column with a letter for the day. I cross'd these columns with thirteen red lines, marking the beginning of each line with the first letter of one of the virtues, on which line, and in its proper column, I might mark, by a little black spot, every fault I found upon examination to have been committed respecting that virtue upon that day.

FORM OF THE PAGES

Temperance

Eat not to dullness; drink not to elevation

	Sun.	M.	T.	W.	Th.	F.	S.
Tem.[perance]							
Sil.[ence]	*	*		*		*	
Ord.[er]	*	*			*	*	*
Res.[traint]		*				*	
Fru.[gality]		*				*	
Ind.[ustry]			*				
Sinc.[erity]							
Jus.[tice]							
Mod.[eration]							
Clea.[nliness]							
Tran.[quility]							
Chas.[tity]							
Hum.[ility]							

I determined to give a week's strict attention to each of the virtues successively. Thus, in the first week, my great guard was to avoid even the least offence against *Temperance*, leaving the other virtues to their ordinary chance, only marking every evening the faults of the day. Thus, if in the first week I could keep my first line, marked T, clear of spots, I suppos'd the habit of that virtue so much strengthen'd, and its opposite weaken'd, that I might venture extending my attention to include the next, and for the following week keep both lines clear of spots. Proceeding thus to the last, I could go thro' a course compleat in thirteen weeks, and four courses in a year. And like him who, having a garden to weed, does not attempt to eradicate all the bad herbs at once, which would exceed his reach and his strength, but works on one of the beds at a time, and, having accomplish'd the first, proceeds to a second, so I should have, I hoped, the encouraging pleasure of seeing on my pages the progress I made in virtue, by clearing successively my lines of their spots, till in the end, by a number of courses, I should be happy in viewing a clean book, after a thirteen weeks' daily examination.

I enter'd upon the execution of this plan for self-examination, and continu'd it with occasional intermissions for some time. I was surpris'd to find myself so much fuller of faults than I had imagined; but I had the satisfaction of seeing them diminish. To avoid the trouble of renewing now and then my little book, which, by scraping out the marks on the paper of old faults to make room for new ones in a new course, became full of holes, I transferr'd my tables and precepts to the ivory leaves of a memorandum book, on which the lines were drawn with red ink, that made a durable stain, and on those lines I mark'd my faults with a black-lead pencil, which marks I could easily wipe out with a wet sponge. After a while I went thro' one course only in a year, and afterward only one in several years, till at length I omitted them entirely, being employ'd in voyages and business abroad, with a multiplicity of affairs that interfered; but I always carried my little book with me.

My scheme of ORDER gave me the most trouble; and I found that, tho' it mght be practicable where a man's business was such as to leave him the disposition of his time, that of a journeyman printer, for instance, it was not possible to be exactly observed by a master, who must mix with the world, and often receive people of business at their own hours. *Order*, too, with regard to places for things, papers, etc., I found extremely difficult to acquire. I had not been early accustomed to it, and, having an exceeding good memory, I was not so sensible of the inconvenience attending want of method. This article, therefore, cost me so much painful attention, and my faults in it vexed me so much, and I made so little progress in amendment, and had such frequent relapses, that I was almost ready to give up the attempt, and content myself with a faulty character in that respect, like the man who, in buying an ax of a smith, my neighbor, desired to have the whole of its surface as bright as the edge. The smith consented to grind it bright for him if he would turn the wheel; he turn'd, while the smith press'd the broad face of the ax hard and heavily on the stone, which made the turning of it very fatiguing. The man came every now and then from the wheel to see how the work went on, and at length would take his ax as it was, without farther grinding. "No," said the smith, "turn on, turn on; we shall have it bright by-and-by; as yet, it is only speckled." "Yes," says the man, *"but I think I like a speckled ax best."* And I believe this may have been the case with many, who, having for want of some such means as I employ'd, found the difficulty of obtaining good and breaking bad habits in other points of vice and virtue, have given up the struggle, and concluded that *"a speckled ax was best"*; for something, that pretended to be reason, was every now and then suggesting to me that such extream nicety as I exacted of myself might be a kind of foppery in morals, which, if it were known, would make me ridiculous; that a perfect character might be attended with the inconvenience of being envied and hated; and that a benevolent man should allow a few faults in himself, to keep his friends in countenance.

In truth, I found myself incorrigible with respect to Order; and now I am grown old, and my memory bad, I feel very sensibly the want of it. But, on the whole, tho' I never arrived at the perfection I had been so ambitious of obtaining, but fell far short of it, yet I was, by the endeavor, a better and a happier man than I otherwise should have been if I had not attempted it; as those who aim at perfect writing by imitating the engraved copies, tho' they never reach the wish'd-for excellence of those copies, their hand is mended by the endeavor, and is tolerable while it continues fair and legible.

My list of virtues contain'd at first but twelve; but a Quaker friend having kindly informed me that I was generally thought proud; that my pride show'd itself frequently in conversation; that I was not content with being in the right when discussing any point, but was overbearing, and rather insolent, of which he convinc'd me by mentioning several instances; I determined endeavoring to cure myself, if I could, of this vice or folly among the rest, and I added *Humility* to my list, giving an extensive meaning to the word.

I cannot boast of much success in acquiring the *reality* of this virtue, but I had a good deal with regard to the *appearance* of it.

Indeed, so hard was it to displace pride by humility, that Franklin notes: "Disguise it, struggle with it, beat it down, stifle it, modify it as much as one pleases, it is so alive, it will every now and then peep out and show itself; you will see it perhaps, often in this history; for, even if I could conceive that I had completely overcome it, I shall probably be proud of my humility." Of course, the development of the *appearance* of the virtue, without success in developing its internal core, may appear to be the grossest hypocrisy. If, on the other hand (as the James-Lange conception of the emotions proclaims) the acts that we carry out send a certain backwash which physiologically affects our consciousness in a specific way, it may be that this, like role-playing, will first achieve the appearance and then gradually the inner workings—apparently a reasonable experiment to try on a larger scale than has yet been attempted.

DARWIN

One of the greatest of self-deceptions remaining to man in the modern era has been the conviction that he stands apart from all other living things. Here a few more words about Charles Darwin may be helpful, for it was he, beyond all others, who drove home the conviction that man is a part of the natural order of the world.

There were, indeed, three giant steps still to be made in the West, to be made by Darwin, Einstein, and Freud. With the Greeks, man had been "the measure of all things"; indeed, in a sense deeper than the Greeks realized, the rational order of the world was given by the social order within which the Greek citizen was ensconced. Thus, Xenophanes had noted that snub-nosed people made and worshiped snub-nosed gods, hawk-nosed people had made hawk-nosed gods, but he did not quite grasp that beyond all these local variations, the order discovered in the world reflected common human assumptions; it was a man-centered, or "anthropocentric," universe in which the Greeks lived. Their own weaknesses and sins were also committed by the Homeric gods. The whole order of nature was a human order. The world not only had to be purposive; it had to be humanly purposive.

The great historical issue here was how the anthropocentric view of the world (in some ways strengthened by both Old and New Testament conceptions of the relation of man to God) could be gradually freed of the deeper assumptions that natural events were reassuringly purposive in a human sense. The blow needed to be directed at the heart of the ancient system. It needed to show, as in the work of Darwin, the relative position of things human among things cosmic. It needed to show man placed in his biological niche within the entire system of biological niches on the face of the earth, and these in relation to the evolution of the earth's crust and the forms of life developing within it. As Copernicus, through personal discipline, worked his way from a less heliocentric to a more heliocentric system, Darwin worked his way from a British middle-class conception of a God-to-man relationship, through slowly and systematically ordering observations in the light of an impersonal theory—a theory constantly modified by fresh observations—and came to see the nature of the human mind as given in the biology of instinct and the learning process. He saw human life in terms of the comparative portraiture of the various forms of lives, simple and complex, of which *human* nature is one advanced manifestation. To achieve this, we might expect a man to need an exceptional amount of skill and humility and direct self-perception—that is, to understand anthropocentrism and the ways of escaping from it and to understand a little about personal egocentricism and self-deception.

Here are some notes by Darwin on his childhood taken from *The Autobiography of Charles Darwin and Selected Letters*, edited by Francis Darwin:

> By the time I went to this day-school my taste for natural history, and more especially for collecting, was well developed. I tried to make out the names of plants, and collected all sorts of things, shells, seals, franks, coins, and minerals. The passion for collecting which leads a man to be a systematic naturalist, a virtuoso, or a miser, was very strong in me, and was clearly innate, as none of my sisters or brother ever had this taste.
>
> One little event during this year has fixed itself very firmly in my mind, and I hope that it has done so from my conscience having been afterward sorely troubled by it; it is curious as showing that apparently I was interested at this early age in the variability of plants! I told another little boy . . . that I could produce variously coloured polyanthuses and primroses by watering them with certain coloured fluids, which was of course a monstrous fable. . . .
>
> I have said that in one respect my mind has changed during the last twenty or thirty years. Up to the age of thirty, or beyond it, poetry of many kinds, such as the works of Milton, Gray, Byron, Wordsworth, Coleridge, and Shelley, gave me great pleasure, and even as a schoolboy I took intense delight in Shakespeare, especially in the historical plays. I have also said that formerly pictures gave me considerable, and music very great, delight. But now for many years I cannot endure to read a line of poetry; . . .

Darwin's mind was shaped into craving certain particular *kinds* of reality. These he learned to emphasize. The public, in turn, had to learn from him something about the scientific way of looking at man, and the sheer weight of a hundred years of further biologic research *still* leaves us "human, all too human" in our ways of looking at our animal ancestry.

The battles against Darwinism in the subsequent years of the nineteenth century were largely battles attempting the restoration of an anthropocentric outlook. Disraeli, at the Oxford Diocesan Conference in 1864, exclaimed, "Is man an ape or an angel? I, my Lord, I am on the side of the angels. I repudiate with indignation and abhorrence those new fangled theories." Not only political prestige but personal gratification were threatened by intellectual honesty, and even a man of high intelligence could simultaneously invoke both against the broadening understanding of the world of science. Darwin could well have employed similar religious and personal defenses, but he declined to do so. Darwinism, with all its many imperfections as a theory, represents a major direction of discovery.

FREUD

As Copernicus helped man to see that his vision of the universe was earthbound, and as Darwin helped man to see that biological perspective had been distorted through a theory of "special creation," so Freud helped man to understand to some degree the biases of all his perception, memory, imagination, and thought powered by his unconscious needs. The process of evasion of reality had to be understood and a "reality principle" discovered.

In the context of our present thought the struggle of Freud to penetrate the vast underworld of unconscious dynamics in human thought has much in common with the effort of Darwin to give comprehensive meaning to tens of thousands of odd bits of biological information. Freud's task was so huge that he kept encountering conflicting evidence, and when a mass of clinical evidence fell into place, it usually led to a new depth, as if there were trapdoors, false bottoms beyond each new discovery. Dr. Max Schur, Freud's personal physician, tells of Freud's long, turbulent preoccupation with the Greek myths of love and death. In *Freud: Living and Dying*, Schur writes:

> In Greek mythology Mnemosyne and Lethe—memory and oblivion—were two springs found at the entrance to the Netherworld. Freud's reference to a draught of punch with Lethe was thus an expression of his longing for some respite from the superhuman task he had undertaken. He had reached the entrance to the lowest world, had

drunk from the spring of Mnemosyne, and was now yearning for a taste of Lethe. But not for long. The inner equilibrium was quickly re-established.

Schur also quotes a letter of Freud that suggests challenging new ideas for later works:

Can you imagine what "endopsychic myths" are? They are the latest product of my mental labours. The dim inner perception of one's own psychical apparatus stimulates illusions, which are naturally projected outward, and characteristically into the future and a world beyond. Immortality, retribution, the world after death, are all reflections of our inner psyche.

For Freud, the mind—the world of memory and thought—is driven largely by the deep motivating forces of the unconscious. This may seem an extravagant generalization, but winnowed and purified by the clinical and experimental study of three-quarters of a century, it seems today to be a *discovery*, which came to Freud because he himself had battled against a formal philosophy that could not penetrate to the depths.

In a very real sense, Freud is a discoverer of huge realities from which man had been excluded. He carved out a new inner world for us to explore, settle, and accept. He persistently battled his own middle-class biases, as well as those common to human society. Post-Victorian Europe at first vehemently scoffed at Freud's findings, but as the early-twentieth-century climate changed, there gradually emerged a willingness to accept his approaches. Just as Darwin shortly before had helped to naturalize man's place in the cosmos, so Freud showed the unconscious to be a natural extension of man's domain, the wellspring of his energies and motivations.

EINSTEIN

Have we now completed the very last of Western man's primary steps toward outgrowing self-deception? Probably not.

We must learn to think the way Einstein did. The men and women of our era, however, are only beginning to understand the implications of Einstein's work and the relativity theory. The phrase we must quote from Einstein is: "There is no privileged position." We have learned from Einstein not only that the descriptions of nature are relative to the observational (and conceptual) systems of the observer but also that without the ground rules of science, observations from a world of the merely apparent cannot be transferred to the world of the really "real." The time taken for an event, the amount of energy that can be released at a particular time and point from atomic fuels, are observable only within a frame of reference beyond which there is no preferable alternative frame of reference. In the same spirit, and advancing a step further, Heisenberg has shown that there is an inherent principle of "uncertainty" in physical observation: the instruments of observation, such as the electron microscope, change the events being observed. More broadly, the location and momentum of a particle cannot be specified at the same time; one of these may be specified, but if that is specified, the other must remain unspecified.

A certain pervasive humility may seem to physicists to require a return to the ancient Greek principle that man is "the measure of all things." But in a far more radical sense, self-deception appears to arise not merely from evolutionary processes, and not only from anthropocentric residues, but from the very nature of science. There are further steps necessary to show even more radically how deeply our best observations are influenced by biases that go to the very core of what we are.

The lives of Darwin, Freud, and Einstein lend us hope that there is actually something new under the sun: the beginnings of a discipline of observation of the world and of man oriented fundamentally toward the discovery and control of self-deception. The Darwinian view helped to show man's outlook as that of another species, the ways in which his evolving path has given him a human orientation toward life lived here on the earth, in the perspective of very necessary self-deceptions.

The human species cannot unlearn the ways of seeing but it can learn to understand more fully that this way of "seeing as man" is fundamentally built into all human structures. Psychoanalysis in turn has taught man that his interpersonal tensions, defenses, conflicts, and struggles toward emancipation will always be with him as he tries to understand the stolid blindness or furious hostility with which he rejects reality. To some degree "where id was, there shall ego be." Yet ego remains rich in deceits while it cultivates the ideal, seeking the "reality principle."

Much more radical is the gradual discovery of the implications of Einstein's relativity principle. These involve much more than the ancient wisdom incarnated in the phrase "all is relative." Einstein's concepts were systematically explored by the augmented sense organs of telescope, spectroscope, and sound recorder and the magnification of sensory skills that we considered in Chapter 2. It recognized a comprehensive system of checks and balances among the many shortages of information, and expresses itself through a mathematics that was applicable to all observers. It recognized the inherent bias in being human but aimed, nevertheless, to find ways of reducing such bias.

ASIAN APPROACHES
TO SELF-UNDERSTANDING

As men in the West, we have drawn upon illustrations of progressive emancipation from the Western world. To emphasize the West has in a way added to our own cultural and personal self-deception. It will, however, have to be a forgivable arrogance. We shall, however, note very briefly that *Asian* cultural history shows some of these same steps.

The gods of the Rig-Veda (1500 B.C.) are essentially human, and in the centuries that led to the great philosophical treatises of the Upanishads, they gave way to a cosmic principle not directly related to the human nature that we see about us. Then followed a discipline, in the various forms of yoga, to advance man's craving for the practical refinement of self-emancipation, which went hand in hand with philosophical refinement, a seeking to purify the man-to-God relationship.

The beautiful song, the Bhagavad-Gita, set in the midst of one of the great epic poems, constantly picks up the refrain of human self-deception through "involvement," "preoccupation," and "commitment" to the passing things of the world we perceive. The only respite from suffering lies in detachment, the process of weaning oneself from vain investment. Buddhism, rejecting much of the earlier Hindu thought, nevertheless preserved and enriched this idea of detachment in later developments such as Zen Buddhism, first in China, then in Japan. It moves toward an absolute serenity which, as in Western Stoicism, allows one to achieve absolute indifference to pleasure and pain. This attitude of detachment had likewise been cultivated over the centuries by the Chinese philosophy of Tao. Indeed, philosophies of detachment, rare and incompletely investigated in the West, pervade all the great Asian systems.

Gautama, the Enlightened One (the Buddha), found difficulty in accepting the reality of a changeless soul and insisted simply on direct observations of the stream of thought, which was to be continued in the thought of a person born later. He sought emancipation through self-discovery. One man, moreover, could help another man, born later, toward such self-discovery, and the wise ones, the Bodhisattvas, could help less-developed individuals toward self-emancipation. When the biasing passions of self-deception are winnowed away, the strifeless soul is born. Cultivation of such strifeless life, as in Zen, while still in the body, marks a high point of the Asian tradition.

Through the explorations of inner psychology and physiology, which we have described in earlier chapters, it appears that the West is beginning to experience and document much that has long been known in the East. At the same time, however, the pertinence of science as it is known in the West is clear. In particular, biological scientists have joined forces with the self-regulation and self-control theorists and practitioners of the East, for they are discovering and systematizing the vast biological backgrounds of consciousness. Physiology may be seen "from an Eastern window" just as yoga and Zen may be seen from a Western window, as one looks in toward the still-obscure inner world of man. We have indeed come full circle; the convergence of Western reality-seeking techniques and of Eastern reality-transcending means of thought and action may be regarded by some as paths converging toward a science of self-discovery.

This is the way the *Western* observer sees it, at least if he has immersed himself for a long time in the ways of science. But, of course, we cannot in this little volume give the reader any fair conception of what the great mystics of the East (Patanjali, for example) and the West (like Plotinus) have meant by *reality*, or rather, the mystic *way* to a "*real* reality." Nor can we explain here why our Western practical reality, as science itself, seems to the mystic to be illusory. The mystic and the scientist ("the Yogi and the Commissar") seem to find some common ground when the scientist is talking but less when the mystic is talking.

Most of us who try to reconcile opponents who are caught in fundamental conflict are rather proud of ourselves for our tolerance. But just as Franklin found that in achieving humility he might be "proud of his humility," so we shall probably find that in achieving the unified view of the self we shall have included in our dish a large measure of self-deception. In keeping with Einstein's principle that "there is no privileged position," there is no pot of gold at the rainbow's end. But we are inclined to accept the reality and the beauty of the rainbow even without the pot of gold.

HOW FAST CAN ONE MOVE?

Every system of ideas, every "establishment," is organized in great depth, as Dr. Johnson said of a "network," "tessellated and reticulated," so that if any part is amiss, the whole collapses. In minor civil controversies, such as over real estate, motorcar accidents, or failure to keep one's sidewalks clear, the issue comes up: "What shall I yield without argument? What shall I admit among the claims of my adversary?" "Nothing at all?" In campaign speeches, one "views with alarm" *every* argument of one's antagonist, because if a single exception is made, the reply is: "He himself admits." Little innocent caveats are allowed and admired among gentlemen, for these show strength in a very real sense, but to begin to attempt seriously to weaken the hold of self-deception upon the heart of man is to show oneself a romantic, a visionary, and, especially, a nuisance.

One can just see the tough-minded getting organized to defend first with laughter, then with a grim petulance, the elementary and sacred right to self-deception. What the freethinkers were to the solid self-respecting Calvinist farmers of yesteryear, what the birth controllers were to the decent people of 1900, what the peaceniks are today to the patriotic masses, these strange people who would like to root out prejudice will be to almost all sane and reasonable men and women. The idea of outgrowing self-deception appears essentially humanly absurd, and if it were not so ridiculous, it would be dangerous. "Since it is essentially a humorless idea, let us destroy it with our laughter." It will not make a dent in this century, and only with great difficulty in the next one. Think of the president or even a congressman saying several times a week, "Of course, I was blind to several major issues on which I made decisions last week; I shall need help. It is an odd feeling to find one's political convictions of today clearly invalidated tomorrow." Or imagine the domestic scene in which family battles are slowly quieted down, with husbands and wives granting that they had missed major points, and that they do not have to be dragged into divorce courts in order to admit their incredible stupidity, or triviality, or meanness. On many occasions the cost will be very, very great. And since by definition any victory along the way will annoy one's comrades, almost as much as it annoys the enemy, there will have to be some very solid satisfactions in view, and some of them very frequently realized if movement along the road is to continue. In fact, the satisfactions will have to be monumental. As in Shaw's *Don Juan in Hell,* the unde-ceived will have to be more interesting than the "normally biased" men and women, who leave us comfortably and guiltlessly alone.

Some years ago a good deal was written about the "bal-anced" or "integrated" personality, on the assumption that if one has a certain amount of one trait, one should have other balancing traits. If one is a little bold, one must also be a little gentle, a little humorous, a little sly; if one is a little dishonest, a little frank. We don't like real lopsidedness—a man who is a creative genius on Tuesdays but an *idiot savant* on Thurs-days. We all need the strength of our weaknesses and the weakness of our strengths. Perhaps the rest of us could hardly bear having too many "good" traits in our opposite numbers. They would humiliate us. We often are like the Athenian citizen who voted to ostracize Aristides because he was tired of hearing him called the "just." The leaner-over-backwards is himself obnoxious most of the time. But what of him who would really move toward the serious reduction of his basic reality distortions? Isn't his self-deception regarded as a lovable characteristic, a gracious charming form of charisma? What, would you take away the humanity of our delightful friend?

A "normal" amount of self-deception is usually laudable. It may be like the amount of pathology that we can "afford." A certain percentage of each person's genes may be defective; a certain number of his abilities may be impaired by childhood diseases or by a disturbing environment. It is a question of how much he (and we) can "tolerate." Perhaps the amount of self-deception to be blinked at or applauded is like the amount of fallout we can tolerate from atomic testing without running "too great" a risk of bone cancer in our children. The optimum amount of self-deception would not be zero, but say 5 percent. This would be the "norm," and those with 2 percent and those with 10 percent would be equally "abnormal." Indeed, at certain levels of adaptation—say of our cavemen ancestors—it may well be that such a fraction of deceit (in all its forms) may have had biological advantages.

Nevertheless, the question arises whether in the complexities of today's industrial society there is any *real* safety in the avoidance of evidence—especially when masses move in unison—whether there is any protection against those biases that are more or less uniform for the group. At the beginning of the twentieth century, when Harvey Wiley campaigned against poisonous foods and drugs, it took only a few clearheaded leaders to overcome the organized crooked thinking of the mass. But during the past few years, the serious threat of pollution of many sorts had to be alarmingly great before the few could begin to convince the many; industry had too much invested in it.

Yes, we might put everyone on a quota for self-deceptive activity, some people thinking straight on Monday, Wednesday, and Friday, others on Tuesday and Thursday, but all easing up, "so as to be human," on evenings and weekends.

[161]

THE POSSIBILITIES OF
THE EXAMINED LIFE

Assuming that the mechanisms exist and will work, that the will to change is present, and that the opportunity for reconditioning exists, there are still great difficulties in the way. In a larger sense it is as if our entire society acts as a drag upon the person who wishes to pursue this kind of change. Albert Schweitzer, in the epilogue to his book *Out of My Life and Thought*, observes:

Thus, his whole life long, the man of today is exposed to influences which are bent on robbing him of all confidence in his own thinking. The spirit of spiritual dependence to which he is called on to surrender is in everything he hears or reads; it is in the people whom he meets every day; it is in the parties and associations which have claimed him as their own; it pervades all the circumstances of his life.

From every side and in the most varied ways it is dinned into him that the truths and convictions which he needs for life must be taken by him from the associations which have rights over him. The spirit of the age never lets him come to himself. Over and over again convictions are forced upon him in the same way as, by means of the electric advertisements which flare in the streets of every large town, any company which has sufficient capital to get itself securely established, exercises pressure on him at every step he takes to induce him to buy their boot polish or their soup tablets. . . .

His self-confidence is also diminished through the pressure exercised upon him by the huge and daily increasing mass of knowledge. He is no longer in a position to take in as something which he has grasped all the new discoveries that are constantly announced; he has to accept them as fact although he does not understand them. This being his relation to scientific truth he is tempted to acquiesce in the idea that in matters of thought also his judgment cannot be trusted.

Nevertheless, it should be possible to see the implications of a life relatively free of self-deception. The prospects begin slowly, in a small circle: spouse, parents, children, friends. A curious kind of detachment can emerge, as one steps beyond the charmed circle of illusion about self and family. Even the tribal views can change, so that one's own community or ethnic group is seen much as any other. The prospects are both fascinating and terrifying. One can possibly surrender allegiance to a small (or larger) piece of turf, seeing a flag as simply one of many possible allegiances.

Ah, but can one surrender the allegiance to an age cohort, with whom one grew up and shared a lifetime's experiences? Is it possible to say, "I was scarred by the Great Depression," then thoroughly examine its full consequences, and then shake them off? Can one see the shortcomings of a given profession's training and the biases that it produces: the hairsplitting of the lawyer or scholar, the constant urge to help of the social worker, the eternal explainer in the teacher?

Can one step outside of one's religion, and say, "Yes, there are truly many roads up the mountain to God," and really begin to perceive the applied implications of such a staggering belief? Protestants and Catholics have indeed taken such steps in their joint biblical historical research. Can one emerge outside of one's race, sex, class, or culture to see the unity that lies inherent in that wonderful, dirty, gregarious, anxious, curious, creative, irritable simian superprimate *Homo sapiens*? Social theorists of organization are able to discern clearly the structural similarities in capitalist and socialist hierarchies. Individuals from upper and lower classes frequently are surprised to discover how much they have in common. The young of today are often intrigued to find that they have more to share with their age peers abroad than they have with their own parents. Is it possible to envision a relatively objective world history, written from multiple points of view, as is postulated in the UNESCO world history project?

Can one, like Schweitzer, step outside of man, and see the unity of living forms, treating chimpanzees and donkeys, parrots and snakes, along with his fellow men, in a hospital of all life? Biological scientists are beginning to think this way but many still lack the *caritas*, the impartial and unselfish love, of a Schweitzer.

The challenge rests in what can be achieved by the genuinely curious and open ones who persist in climbing the final Everests of self-knowledge and being.

ADDITIONAL READINGS

In the Chapter 8 discussion of the various techniques for overcoming self-deception, there are a number of references that can be followed up, if the reader is so inclined. Some of these are classics, well worth reading in their own right, as entrees to great, creative, and thoughtful minds. We have restricted this brief discussion to those publications currently available.

For Freud, it is far better to read him than to read about him. Two works extremely useful here are *The Interpretation of Dreams*, translated by James Strachey (New York: Basic Books, 1955); and his *New Introductory Lectures on Psychoanalysis*, edited and translated by James Strachey (New York: Norton, 1965). A follow-up book, meaningful in this context, is Anna Freud's *The Ego and the Mechanisms of Defense*, revised edition (New York: International Universities Press, 1967).

The discussion of integrating analytic thinking with feedback thinking is best presented in Chapter VI of *Gestalt Therapy: Excitement and Growth in the Human Personality*, by Frederick Perls, Ralph Hefferline, and Paul Goodman (New York: Julian Press, 1969). A related very current statement on this theme is Barbara B. Brown's *New Mind, New Body Bio-Feedback: New Directions for the Mind* (New York: Harper and Row, 1974).

Jung's most complete statement of philosophy may be found in his warm and delightful *Memories, Dreams, Reflections*, translated by R. and C. Winston (New York: Pantheon Books, 1973).

An early discussion by Carl R. Rogers appears in his *Client Centered Therapy* (Boston: Houghton Mifflin, 1951). A later version may be found in his *On Becoming a Person* (Boston: Houghton Mifflin, 1970).

A concise summary of yoga, may be found in the section on yoga, "The Psychology of India," in *Asian Psychology*, edited by Gardner and Lois Murphy (New York: Basic Books, 1968). A similar summary may be found farther on in the same book, in the section on Zen Buddhism, under "The Psychology of Japan." Anything written by D. T. Suzuki on Zen is useful, but the best anthology of his work is edited by Bernard Phillips, *The Essentials of Zen Buddhism: An Anthology of the Writings of Daisetz T. Suzuki* (Westport, Conn.: Greenwood, 1973).

Harry Stack Sullivan's views may be located in his *Collected Works*, 2 volumes (New York: Norton, 1953–1964), but especially in volume 1, *Interpersonal Theory of Psychiatry* (1953).

Jacob L. Moreno's concepts are detailed in two books: *Psychodrama*, 3 volumes, and *Who Shall Survive* (Beacon, N.Y.: Beacon House, 1946–1969). *Psychodrama* is more specific for this context, providing the details of his dramatic theory and practice.

D. Berlyne's discussion of curiosity, as well as his broader outlook, appears in his *Structure and Direction in Thinking* (New York: John Wiley & Sons, 1965).

Encounter and sensitivity groups have exploded so rapidly that it is difficult to keep up with what has become a major social movement in the field of psychology. Very useful here is a statement of one of the key early figures of the field, Carl Rogers, who has assembled a short book, *Carl Rogers on Encounter Groups* (New York: Harper & Row, 1973). Useful in a different way is a new study, *Encounter Groups: First Facts*, by M. A. Lieberman, D. Yalom, and M. B. Miles (New York: Basic Books, 1973), offering the beginnings of research into encounter. A more typical statement exists in W. B. Schutz's *Joy: Expanding Human Awareness* (New York: Grove, 1967).

PERMISSIONS

INDEX

Index

Index

Index